Y0-BYV-062

AI Theory and Applications in the VAX Environment

Michael Stock

Q335
S85
1988

Intertext Publications
McGraw-Hill Book Company
New York, N.Y.

To Leonardo Da Vinci
— the ultimate Knowledge Engineer

Library of Congress Catalog Card Number 87-83097

10 9 8 7 6 5 4 3 2 1

ISBN 0-07-061573-X (paperback)
ISBN 0-07-061574-8 (hardcover)

Intertext Publications/Multiscience Press, Inc.
McGraw-Hill Book Company
1221 Avenue of the Americas
New York, NY 10020

Knowledge Craft is a trademark of Carnegie Group.
VAX, VAX LIST, VAX OPS5, CMS, MMS, VMS, DECNET, Rdb, FMS, DATATRIEVE, MICROVAX, DEC, TDMS, UIS, and DBMS are all trademarks of Digital Equipment Corp.
ART is a trademark of Inference Corp.
KEE is a trademark of Intellicorp.
Nexpert Objects is a trademark of Neurondata.
S1 is a trademark of Tecknowledge.

Contents

Acknowledgements

With great appreciation and much devotion I wish to acknowledge the input, support and help by the following individuals:

Mr. and Mrs. Edward Stock, my loving and supportive parents.

My loving wife, Rose Stock.

My three sons, Michael, Christopher, and Jonathan.

Marvin Berlin, co-founder of Artificial Intelligence Technologies.

Patricia Sullivan, who performed the administrative and secretarial functions necessary to develop this work.

All the other technical people who have dramatically affected my thought processes on these and very many other industrial and technical matters.

Preface

As an architect, designer, and implementer, I have been involved in state-of-the-art technology for well over 18 years. During that time, I have concentrated on developing leading edge methodologies that can allow truly intelligent systems to be built for mainstream industrial environments. The concepts, methodologies, techniques, and tools contained in this book are novel and represent my thoughts on a scientific methodology for building intelligent applications on traditional computing architectures.

Moreover, the concepts and methodologies that are contained in this book, such as integrated artificial intelligence, cooperating expert systems, distributed artificial intelligence, domain-specific solution shells, and time-critical AI, have been found to be essential when addressing tough knowledge-based problems on traditional architectures such as the VAX computing environment.

This book covers the above topics, as well as many others, in detail and should provide a firm intellectual and engineering foundation for creative and industrial-strength products, projects, and services in this technology area. Moreover, *AI Theory and Applications in the VAX Environment* represents the first in a series of books to be called the "Intelligent Technology Series." The goal of this series is to provide a firm, well-documented scientific foundation for the continuing evolution of technology in the area of intelligent systems.

1

Introduction:
What Is Artificial Intelligence?

There has been much debate about what exactly constitutes artificial intelligence (AI). One view is that there are certain signposts associated with AI, but that the presence or absence of any one signpost does not determine whether or not the process is AI. It merely indicates that the problem might contain a large nontraditional computing component (see Figure 1-1).

AI can be viewed as a collection of tools, concepts, techniques, and methodologies that allows certain problems to be addressed that cannot be easily modeled in a closed-form analytic solution. It can also be viewed as a way of attacking a problem for which there is not a rational design center without AI or as a way of increasing the design center of an existing problem whose solution was not really satisfactory. This definition is very simple, but it dramatically demystifies the concept of the whole discipline.

Many techniques are used to make the building of intelligent reasoning systems (see Figure 1-2) feasible in realistic time frames with proper software engineering practices. AI is not magic, and it is these techniques along with software environments that translate what seems to be magic into actual step-and-repeat methodological approaches. There are an abundance of myths and realities associated with AI. This book will attempt to cover many issues in their generic

- No closed form analytic representation
- Objects other than formulas and numbers
- Non-determinism
- Search
- Loose algorithm
- Capturing skill
- Learning
- Explanation
- Self modification
- Data driven computation
- Fuzzy reasoning

Figure 1-1 The signposts of Artificial Intelligence.

form with particular references to how they might be exploited intelligently and in an industrially accepted fashion in the VAX computing environment.

Expert Systems and Knowledge-Based Approaches

There has been much discussion over expert systems and knowledge-based approaches. Expert systems are not new to computing. Without expert systems, computerization would not be as pervasive as it is today. There are really two types of expert systems: one that has heuristic AI content associated with it and another that does not. If a problem can be described by a set of simultaneous linear equations, it can be solved by using Gauss Siedel's method and a wholly satisfactory expert system can be obtained. This expert system, however, does not have any explicit heuristic content. Yet, it is expert in what it does. There are fundamental differences, however, between the architecture, design, and implementation on a VAX of an expert system with heuristic content and one without it.

There also has been much discussion about knowledge-based systems and techniques. The spirit of what knowledge-based systems attempt to describe is as follows. All forms of computerization are comprised of a few types of information and funtionality. They are control, data, representation, and application kernel program logic (see Figure

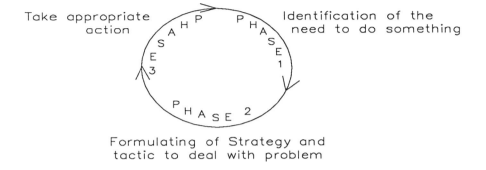

Take appropriate action

Identification of the need to do something

Formulating of Strategy and tactic to deal with problem

Figure 1-2 The intelligent reasoning cycle.

1-3). In traditional computing approaches these four things are treated very differently from an architecture and a design viewpoint and as an implementation vehicle. The goal of true knowledge-based systems is to not differentiate between any of these components and to have them all reflected declaratively in the declarative component of a knowledge base. In traditional programming, once a function is compiled away, it is very difficult for other code fragments to determine its existence, let alone to modify it. However, if that code fragment was not merely compiled away but was represented and modeled declaratively as data, or knowledge, and at any point instantiated as a particular version of itself, the foundation has been set to reason about how one reasons.

The Signposts of AI

There are many fields that have not been recognized as being AI or part of AI that have a tremendous heuristic flavor about them. They include much of applied math, numerical analysis, operations research, and systems analysis. Many of the AI signposts and even some of the techniques that are used to solve heuristic-content problems that have an expert component or knowledge-based orientation occur in time-tested operations research methodologies and solutions. Some of the many signposts associated with the potential presence of a

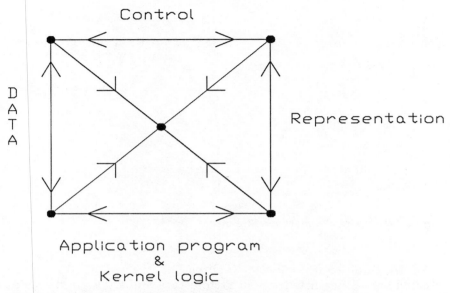

Figure 1-3 The components of intelligence.

heuristic content in a particular problem that needs to be solved in a industrial fashion follow.

The first signpost is an inability to describe a problem using a closed-form analytic solution. This is very important. What it says is that a collection of formulas cannot totally model what you are trying to do in a way that you can functionally and analytically arrive at a solution (i.e., there is no resultant f = ma).

Another is that the system must mimic certain qualities that are normally associated with the way human beings function. These might take the form of the systems' ability to learn, to explain how it does what it does, to exhibit some reasoning based on broad under-standing, and to focus experience, skill, and knowledge very precisely on a particular aspect of the problem at just the right time. Charac-teristics like this are difficult to realize with traditional computing ap-proaches.

A third signpost is the ability or the need to search, which is some-what related to not being able to find a closed-form analytic solution. In order to arrive at a solution to a problem, there must be an algo-rithm. If there is no algorithm, the problem cannot be solved.

However, to the extent that you have to search, and as you have to search more and more, the less well-defined the problem is from an analytic mathematical viewpoint.

An interesting signpost is the observation that a problem is comprised of entities or objects other then numbers and equations. In all the years that I have been building expert systems, knowledge-based applications, and the like, I have never come across a problem that did not have a substantial numerical and formula content to it. However, in every problem for which I ended up relying on AI paradigms, tools, and methodologies and developing new ones, a substantial portion of the problem dealt with the nature of objects and the relationships between objects. Moreover, much of the decision-making process revolved around objects and their relationships to each other. The more nonnumerical data and association, the clearer the signpost that there is a large and lurking AI content.

The next signpost, although very computer-sciency in implementation flavor, is very important in properly architecting, designing, and implementing systems. A very important component to heuristic and knowledge-based systems lies in the fact that although you have an algorithm with which to solve the problem, that algorithm does not easily lend itself to traditional logic-driven programing environments. In traditional logic-driven programming environments, we are confronted with designing an application by which the logic finds the data. To be able to do this, you have to be able to anticipate and design up front every path and to trace through the application. However, many of the heuristic environments that rely on inference-engine-based technology or object-oriented programming techniques have an exact inversion. The data finds the logic. This is commonly referred to as data-driven computation.

What it comes down to is that if you have to implement a particular piece of funtionality that is in line with a particular heuristic signpost, the level of effort needed to do this is less in a heuristic environment then in a traditional computing one. This is an important point. Essentially there are many signposts associated with AI. These signposts impose certain paradigms of computation to intelligently address certain functionality, and heuristic environments give you the paradigms that easily allow you to implement the observed signposts in a particular problem. It's just as simple as that.

Figure 1-1 gives a more complete list of the signposts associated with AI that I have personally experienced and found meaningful over the years.

Tools, Techniques, and Methodologies

Throughout the balance of this book, we will cover a great many of the tools, techniques, and methodologies of AI, many of which are not commonly described in any literature. Here are five of them: integrated AI, cooperating expert systems, distributed AI, time-critical AI, and domain-dependent solution shell technology. These five areas are absolutely essential in addressing real-world industrial-strength problems with a VAX in many application domains. Brief descriptions of these five areas follow (see Figure 1-4).

Integrated AI

Integrated AI is the set of tools, concepts, techniques, and methodologies that combines traditional computing with heuristic computing. The goal is to use the right tool for the right piece of the problem to intelligently combine communications, databases, inferencing, number crunching, graphics, and interfaces.

Cooperating Expert Systems

Cooperating expert systems is the science of breaking up a problem into multiple peer reasoning agents. Historically, the approach has

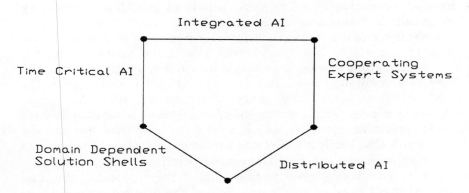

Figure 1-4 New methodologies in Artificial Intelligence.

been the big expert system: lots of schemas and rules until the problem seems solved and then deployment. More often then not, the end result is an unmanageable and costly-to-maintain blob of capability. In cooperating expert systems, we find intelligent ways to decompose the problem and to use methodologies and techniques to resolve the potential conflicts in decision making that might occur. Cooperating expert systems is a key architectural platform from which to address large-scale problems using a VAX.

Distributed AI

I have many Stockisms. One of them is: He or she who lives by the single CPU model dies by the single-CPU model. Distributed AI allows the relaxation of the single-CPU constraint and intelligently and effectively uses any arbitrary collection of VAX computational elements interconnected through any arbitrary collection of communication paths. Distributed AI, as a philosophy and implementation goal, is a very synergistic concept with cooperating expert systems. With the big expert system, there are strategies for distribution, but also the limitation to the inferential component residing on a single machine. If, however, the problem is broken up into five cooperating agents, the inferential component can be naturally and easily distributed over five processers. Also, there are other requirements and opportunities for distribution in addition to simply distributing the inferential component. One would be distributing the computational environment in general. Most problems require traditional databases, number crunching, and graphics interfaces along with heuristic reasoning. This combination becomes an opportunity for intelligent distribution and the use of cooperating agents.

Time-Critical AI

Time-critical AI is essential to many industries. It is the ability to model declaratively and functionally the underlying time and problem constants and to reflect this in the fundamental reasoning process of the expert system. A key question is how intelligent can you afford to be? The synergistic question is how intelligent do you have to be? The balance between these two with a VAX is time-critical AI. According to Stock's maxims, there are no static problems. Take the often maligned payroll application. Most people would say this is a problem without dynamics — it is batch. However, if you used integrated AI techniques to build a super-intelligent payroll system that was a week late with the checks to your company, you would be rudely awakened to the underlying dynamics that are really involved. The methodologies associated with time-critical AI reconcile these issues in a fashion that is tractable in general and in particular with a VAX.

Domain-Dependent Solution Shells

Historically, industry has been building and delivering one-shot expert systems. In plant no. 117 on process A on Tuesday afternoon at three o'clock the expert system does what it is supposed to do. But God help you if you try to use it in plant no. 118 on process C on Wednesday at four o'clock. The thrust behind a domain-dependent solution shell is to architect, design, and implement a flexible, parametric, and knowledge-driven application that can be field installed easily at many sites. Essentially, it is an integrated AI approach to building a fifth-generation application generator. For instance, one type of domain-dependent solution shell might be a shell that schedules. Upon showing up at a particular site, the enduser enters into a dialogue with the shell, easily implanting in the knowledge base the site-specific goals, data, configuration, objectives, and rules. This simple knowledge acquisition phase gives the expert system the knowledge parameters needed to address the problems at that particular site. The great opportunity in AI today is building domain-dependent solution shells to solve problems that have some breadth, as well as depth, in a given vertical market area.

Myths and Realities

There are many myths associated with AI. Here are some of them:

1. If a so-called heuristic product in being used, the process is AI. Nothing could further from the truth. You can sit down with LISP, or any other common expert system development shell, and develop and implement the solution to a set of simultaneous linear equations. This has nothing to do with AI; it is merely using that platform, not using the paradigms of reasoning.

Another myth is that in order to have a true AI system, the thing has to learn, explain itself, and all the rest. Addressing and implementing a solution to a problem that has only one of the many possible signposts reflected in it gives that application a true AI orientation. I have yet to encounter a problem that can be solved using 100 percent AI. In an industrial-strength system the overall AI content is a fraction of the total.

2. AI is built around incremental development. The reality is that there are many levels and types of AI applications. There are small knowledge systems, large expert systems, and humungous expert systems with time-critical reasoning needs. Incremental development seems to be most beneficial when applied to a small knowledge system with a couple of hundred rules, a couple of hundred objects at the most. As problems get larger, it takes a subtle combination of traditional software engineering and systems analysis along with incremental rapid prototyping techniques to deliver a mantainable, verifiable, and on-spec expert system application with AI content.

3. You cannot do true AI or complicated AI on a VAX. The reality could not be further from that statement. What becomes key with a VAX is understanding how to use the five methodological areas that are indicated above. These areas, while general paradigms of computation and general methodologies of architecting and designing systems, become particularly important when applied to traditional computing environments like the VAX.

4. You can develop on one system and easily deliver on another system. This is in direct conflict with another Stock maxim, which I believe is a practical industrial reality, Thou shalt develop on what thy will deliver on.

5. If the expert system has true heuristic content, somehow we do not care about other issues that we have come to assume as standards of excellence with traditional computing technology. Although this is often relied on, again, nothing could be further from the truth. Industry requires the ability to maintain the applications that are deployed. It is essential to have a strategy for the verification and validation of anything that is put into deployment. In addition, most of industrial America requires a phased implementation approach. No one is going to turn over their entire corporation or plant to an untested and untried capability. Knowledge-based approaches to problems must fulfill

all of the standards we associate with high-quality industrial-strength traditional applications plus all the other issues that are imposed because we have used heuristic modeling, methodologies, and implementation techniques with traditional computing approaches.

6. You need a LISP machine to do good AI and to obtain the necessary performance and reasoning funtionality. Although these platforms, when appropriately used, provide excellent capabilities, this attitude, with respect to the traditional computers, is completely and totally without foundation. As a matter of fact, in solving real-world problems, you end up most of the time fighting horrendous battles to integrate the symbolic computational environments with the overall computing environment. This problem is greatly alleviated by staying totally within a traditional computing environment.

7. There are good tools and there are bad tools, good computers and bad computers. Actually, there are different problems with different goals. And what constitutes a good tool or a good computer varies greatly depending upon the characteristics of the problem and the requirements of the solution. Simplistic answers are dangerous in the context of architecting, designing, and implementing state-of-the-art expert systems that are driven with integral knowledge-base approaches.

Conclusion

Throughout the balance of this book we will explore in much greater detail the above technologies and issues, as well as many others. I would like to end this chapter with one final Stock maxim: In simplicity there is genius; unfortunately, very few things are really simple and very few of us really geniuses.

2

Integrated Artificial Intelligence

The Paradigm

Over the years I have developed many expert systems and pioneered many methodologies and paradigms of intelligent computation. Very early in my career I began to realize that there were very few problems that could be solved using only AI or only traditional computing methods. Most problems required a subtle combination of the two. Integrated AI is the paradigm of computation that fosters using the right tool and the right methodology for the right piece of the problem. It is combining the best of traditional computing with the best of symbolic computing to create an intelligent and efficient computation. There are many traditional computing languages and tools and symbolic environments and tools that exist today and that can be used in integrated AI, and the VAX provides an ideal platform for this type of computing.

Benefits of a Solution Machine Approach

Real-World Applications

The need for integrated AI is particularly important in real-world applications. There is a vast difference between prototyping and showing feasibility and delivering an application. Real-world applications require a high degree of integration between mainstream computing and the problem-solving environments in which AI can be most beneficial. Real-world applications must tie intelligently into foreign computers and existing databases, and they must be capable of making use of an installed base of applications and equipment while providing an intelligent solution to problems that have been poorly solved or ignored in the past (see Figure 2-1). The real world is not comprised of islands of automation, but rather is a subtle interchange of data, control, and decision making. Only with the techniques of integrated AI can the coupling necessary to deploy systems that will maximize the benefit to users be accomplished.

The use of a particular programming environment does not in itself qualify as AI; rather, AI is the implementation of the paradigm of computation. If you invert a 100 by 100 matrix in LISP, this in itself does not mean that you are using AI. More than that, if you implement an inference engine in C and use it to heuristically search a decision-making space in a data-driven mode of computation, the fact that your underlying compiler is C does not mean that you are not using AI. Integrated AI, in general and in the VAX computing world in particular, does not lessen the meaningfulness of the AI portion of the computation. Rather, it sets a firm architectural, design, and implementation foundation on which this technology can meet real-world industrial requirements. It is only by coupling LISP with inference engines such as OPS5 (from Digital Equipment Corporation) and ART (from Inference Corporation), using traditional programming languages like Fortran and C tightly integrated with relational databases such as Rdb, and intelligently using communications such as DECnet that we can begin to capture the requirements of most real-world problems. Over the years, the number of tools, both heuristic and traditional, that I have used to address state-of-the-art problems has varied greatly. This is not uncharacteristic of most problems, and in the VAX world it is a decided strength that the architecture and software base lends itself to this type of solution.

Using Integrated AI with VAX

The VAX is not a LISP machine or a OPS5 machine or a C machine; the VAX is a solutions machine. To sit down in front of a VAX, any VAX, and view its architecture, function, and design as a LISP

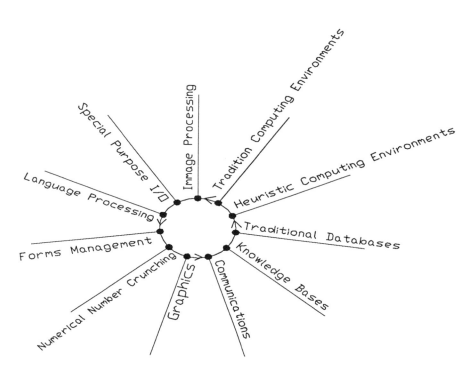

Figure 2-1 The components of integrated AI.

machine is to make a big mistake. This not to say that there are not excellent LISPs, including Digital Equipment Corporation's VAX LISP, which runs on the full range of VAX-based processors. It is to say that the VAX has not been designed for any one type of computation. Rather, it has been designed for many paradigms of computation. It is only by using the right tool for the right piece of the problem that high performance and efficient solutions can be obtained in this computational environment. A fringe benefit to this philosophy is the ability to build very large and complicated systems while significantly reducing the level of effort. Try to find as many components as you can off the shelf. The problems I have tackled over the years have been extraordinarily complicated, have had many ways to go wrong, and have required large engineering efforts to produce anything functional at all. By using integrated AI on the VAX, I have been able to dramatically reduce the cost and the time needed for development and deployment.

Tools, Techniques, and Methodologies

Operating System to the Application

There are many tools, techniques, and methodologies associated with the philosophy of computation that is defined as integrated AI. In the architecture, design, and implementation of an AI application, there are many tools to use such as C, a traditional programming language; VAX LISP, a symbolic programming language; ART, an inference engine (the automated reasoning tool); Rdb, Digital's relations database; FMS, Digital's forms management system; GKS, Digital's device independent graphics system; and, for example, DECnet, Digital's local area communication protocol. These tools must be combined in some intelligent fashion to solve the problem under discussion. One way to do this is to use a methodology that is very important in the proper structuring and architecture of a system: the definition of a new operating system that sits on top of VMS. I like to call this the "operating system to the application." (See Figure 2-2.) All symbolic and traditional programming services are coordinated, integrated, and dispatched intelligently by the operating system to the application that sits on top of VMS. It provides not just a software engineering interface to the developer, but an integrated AI interface to all the developers.

There are many idiosyncratic behavior patterns associated with the different heuristic tools and programming environments. For example, most layered software products and programming environments for VAX adhere to the VMS calling standard that implies that the results of multiple computation environments can be linked into a single resolved runnable object. This statement is not true with respect to LISP on a VAX. LISP generates files that do not conform to the normal VMS calling standards. From VAX LISP, you can call out to another routine, but from a foreign routine you cannot call in.

Architecturally, one very powerful and flexible way that can be used to integrate many facilities is to develop and define the underlying operating system to the application as a transaction or message-

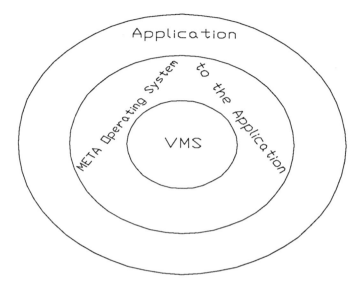

Figure 2-2   An intelligent operating system to the application.

oriented layer. Although a particular resource or function written in LISP cannot be linked, that code fragment can be sent a transaction that describes a certain unit of work to be performed, with the results of that symbolic computation returned to the operating system to the application for further processing. Transaction-oriented processing not only aids dramatically in the building of distributed AI systems, but it lends itself very nicely to developing systems with high availability and fault tolerant characteristics. These details will be enumerated in later chapters. Suffice it to say that given some of the idiosyncrasies of some of the symbolic environments, integration does not always imply a single resolved shareable image, and in most cases it does not apply.

Integrating in the VAX Environment

There are many ways to integrate in the VAX environment. Some of these methods are through shared functionality and some are through data, but most are through control. Architecting an overall application in terms of a client server paradigm and embodying the intelligence to manipulate this paradigm in the operating system to the application resolves many of the idiosyncratic difficulties that occur with the various computational environments. With LISP as it applies to the VAX, there is a Define External Routine command. This command allows the definition of the interface between the VAX LISP environment and a code fragment or piece of functionality external to the LISP system. It is through the proper use of this command and its incorporation in a meaningful sense in the operating system to the application that one can tightly integrate VAX LISP code fragments with the rest of the computational environment.

Relational Databases

Some of the reasons for integrated AI go beyond ease of development and performance to simply overcoming the inefficiencies found in most of the symbolic computational environments. All of the readily found inference engines on the VAX, as well as the general-purpose symbolic environments such as LISP or Prolog, execute in the virtual address space of the computer. On a VAX this implies about 1.1 gigabytes in user mode. One fundamental question is, What if your expert system requires 2 gigabytes? What do you do? In addition, what if you have an environment in which you cannot afford a malfunction of the machine to prohibitively delay computation on the problem. In integrated AI, the answer is to tightly couple traditional databases with the heuristic programming environments and with the underlying application that is being automated. One of the best choices for this tight integration is a relational database. Digital has an outstanding one in Rdb.

The study of relational database theory and the theory of declarative knowledge representation in a knowledge base produces a few important key conclusions: A relational database defines an algebra. A knowledge base whose declarative component is comprised of such things as schemas, semantic nets, or inheritance taxonomies also defines an algebra. The declarative component of the knowledge base can be mapped onto a set of relations and fields in a relational database such as Rdb. Because of this Rdb provides an ideal platform to implement a stable storage architecture in an integrated AI format in the VAX computing environment.

It is possible to forward chain out of the expert system into the relational database to bring new information in and update the database with new decisions that have been made, to backward chain out, or do any combination of the two. The key point is that coupling relational databases into the architecture of the expert system relaxes many of the constraints that are imposed by the symbolic environments that are readily available to the VAX today. A database such as Rdb provides other functionality that is important in integrated AI applications such as journaling, logging, and report writing. In addition, Rdb is transaction oriented — a very important concept to building very sophisticated expert systems on the VAX.

In most applications it is useful to view the facilities provided by Rdb as the global knowledge base and the facilities provided by a tool such as OPS5 or NEXPERT Object (Neuron Data) as the local knowledge base, or as the in-memory knowledge base. You should make sure that everything that is going on in the application is represented in the global knowledge base. This includes control, data, representation, and application kernel program logic. In many ways most intelligent applications can be viewed as a sophisticated MIS system with intelligent expert subroutines operating against the global knowledge base to make decisions. In general, this paradigm is 180 degrees out of phase with the traditional architectures that most people have developed. In those architectures the in-memory knowledge base is the driving force and everything else is a slave computational resource. Sometimes that traditional model is still appropriate. However, the alternate model presented here is a more flexible and stable format for building an extensible system.

User Interfaces

User interfaces are key to the acceptance and usability of any application, particularly one with an intelligent expert component. In integrated AI, there are many resources and layered products that are already available on the VAX. They comprise such aspects as graphics imaging packages, forms management packages, report writing packages, and query facilities. By the appropriate manipulation of these packages from symbolic code fragments, very advanced user interfaces can not only be put together rapidly, but they can be made highly intelligent. For instance, using GKS, the device independent graphics package from Digital; FMS, the forms management system; and even a package such as DATATRIEVE; a database interface and query facility with VAX LISP greatly aids in quickly building sophisticated and intelligent user interfaces.

LISPification

Whether the problem is to overcome the limitations of existing symbolic tools or to use existing applications, code fragments, or databases, the advantages, in terms of time to development and sophistication of the end application of integrated AI, are overpowering. There are other benefits to this approach. One stems from the symbolification of a layered software package or application. For example, to integrate VAX LISP with a package such as GKS or FMS, there is a useful concept called "LISPification." In it all of the facilities of the underlying software package on an existing application or existing database are appropriately LISPified through the use of the Define External Routine function. This means that all of the primitives that exist in that package are now defined as primitives within the VAX LISP environment adhering to common LISP syntax and standards. In the same way, the same functionality can be performed with other symbolic environments such as Prolog or OPS5, to name a few. Essentially, it is making the package a part of the functional capabilities of the symbolic environment. Taking VAX LISP as an example, when a given layered software package has been LISPified, that package can be used and manipulated without leaving the symbolic environment. In the case of graphics, GKS still handles the screen, but the logic, the reasoning behind what is being imaged, when it's being imaged, how it's being imaged, and why it's being imaged is being provided from code fragments in the VAX LISP environment.

You can accomplish several things through the LISPification, OPSification, or ARTification of any layered software package and application. Once you have defined that external facility in your symbolic environment, not only can you use it in a straightforward fashion, but you can reason about it. This is very important in building highly intelligent expert systems, whether they are of a planning, design, a computer-aided instruction nature. By the appropriate LISPification of Rdb, you can reason about which database to use, when to use it, how best to use it, and you can use it, read from it, write to it, and the like.

Conclusion

The key behind integrated AI is to reserve the true open algorithmic reasoning component for the symbolic environment and to use whatever other facilities are needed to accomplish a high-performance, efficient implementation in the minimum time. The VAX computing environment is an ideal one in which to adopt this philosophy.

When you begin a project, you are first concerned with figuring out exactly what the problem is and what functionality you need to provide to solve that problem. Once you have answers to those questions, you should develop an architecture and a mapping of your functionality onto a set of tools. In general, use as much of the philosophy of integrated AI as possible. There are some disadvantages to this philosophy of computation. Obviously, every tool and facility that is incorporated in the design center of a project or product comes with the burden of learning that tool. In addition, the more layered products used, the greater the ultimate run-time cost of the system due to licensing fees. Given these two fundamental drawbacks, you will find that in almost every meaningful product and project that you will be involved with that has an AI component, the advantages associated with an integrated AI approach will greatly outweigh the disadvantages.

I feel so strongly about integrated AI that I have a maxim associated with it. The philosophy of computation, the underlying design center, is a priori that of integrated AI unless through the development of the project or product we can prove otherwise. This Stock maxim is very much akin to the law of our land in which an individual is innocent until proven guilty. I fundamentally believe that integrated AI is a necessity in order to build industrial-strength products that have all of the characteristics and features that are important in any traditional application and in order to do so in an intelligent fashion, minimizing development costs and risks.

In every symbolic computation environment there are mechanisms for being able to enter, as well as exit, that environment. If those entry and exit points are used in either a transaction sense or a message sense or a simple slave computational resource sense, the project is likely to be successful.

3

Cooperating Expert Systems

The Paradigm

Cooperating expert systems represent a philosophy of computation and AI as much as they represents a methodology to accomplish modularity and other system characteristics. Over the last few years, most expert systems have been architected, designed, and implemented as the big expert system model of the world (see Figure 3-1). This means that you begin to prototype and start adding in incremental knowledge. A few schemes are added, a few rules are added. Then, a few more schemes and a few more rules are added. The prototype is reviewed. If the review seems to be successful, more declarative knowledge in the form of schemes and more procedural knowledge in the form of rules are continually added until there is a deployable system implementing an acceptable solution to the design center. This is, by and large, a very unmaintainable, unmodular knowledge base. The alternative to this one-shot big expert system approach is the use of cooperating expert systems, in which the problem is broken up into multiple agents that can function with either the presence or the absence of any other agent (see Figure 3-2).

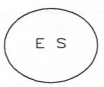

ES = Decision Space & Knowledge Space
& Control Space

Figure 3-1 The single expert system model approach.

Benefits of a Cooperating Expert System

When approaching a problem, it is easy to identify a number of real-world issues that would provide the motivation and determination to build an application that is a set of cooperating expert systems instead of the single big expert system. Some of the motivations are as follows:

1. In the real world very few people will allow an all-or-nothing approach to intelligent automation. For instance, in a computer-integrated manufacturing (CIM) application, it is unlikely that an expert system that is the complete answer to CIM is going to be implemented. Most endusers, if they are organizations doing the development themselves, would rather implement and bring on-line a piece of the solution at a time.

2. In addition, not everyone will necessarily want all of the functionality and knowledge that potentially could be in the knowledge base.

3. By breaking up the problem into multiple agents, there is a better chance of having a number of people working on the expert system at the same time. Essentially, parallel development on these cooperating agents, using certain methodologies, can ensue under fairly close software engineering guidelines. This is not necessarily the case with the big expert system approach in which all of the schemes and all of the rules are contained in the same process.

4. The size of the expert system itself is also a factor. All of the shells that exist today execute in the virtual address space of the computer. There are severe space limitations in any comput-

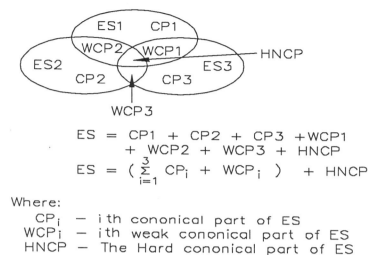

$$ES = CP1 + CP2 + CP3 + WCP1$$
$$+ WCP2 + WCP3 + HNCP$$
$$ES = (\sum_{i=1}^{3} CP_i + WCP_i) + HNCP$$

Where:

CP_i — ith cononical part of ES
WCP_i — ith weak cononical part of ES
HNCP — The Hard cononical part of ES

Figure 3-2   Restructuring ES into a set of three cooperating expert systems.

ing environment, including VAX's. For instance, on the VAX there is roughly 1 gigabyte of virtual address space that can be used in user mode. What do you do if your knowledge base is larger than 1 gigabyte?

5. Additionally, if you have designed the single big expert system, you do not have entities that you can distribute in some intelligent fashion over the network. This limits your ability to make intelligent use of multiple CPUs in a distributed AI fashion.

Conflict Resolution

The paradigm of cooperating expert systems is very akin to the model presented by an Athenian oligarchy in which we have a number of citizens, each with a function in life of trying to help legislate civilization over the community. In the big expert system approach there is always conflict resolution. What do you do if you have more than one rule on the agenda that is ready to fire? Which rule do you choose for processing? There are many traditional techniques in AI to deal with conflict resolution such as specitivity ordering, data ordering, context ordering, priorities, declarative agendas, and scheduling according to rule-set functionality in the procedural component of the knowledge base. When we move to the cooperating expert system model, we encounter the issue of conflict resolution inside of any expert system as well as conflict resolution across expert systems. Now the question becomes, What do you do if expert system A says yes and expert system B says no? How do you continue intelligent decision making and processing to arrive at an overall solution to your problem?

When you approach a problem, the first task at hand is the decomposition of the problem along some functional or task guidelines into the boundaries of the cooperating expert system. For instance in an intelligent CIM application you might decide that there is an order entry agent, a scheduling agent, and a production control agent. If this decomposition results in never having any potential interagent conflicts, you really do not have a cooperating expert system; you have three parallel expert systems. In most problems that I have worked on over the years, this has never been the case. Expert system A depends in some sense, be it in data or decision or control, on expert system B and vica versa. It is not necessarily the case that every agent will depend in some way on every other agent. The dependency can be weaker than that.

When the decision and functionality spaces in a big expert system model are decoupled along some application guidelines, it becomes apparent that in any expert system there are three types of knowledge. The first type is a cononical part in which the decisions that result from that knowledge are not affected by and do not affect any of the other agents in the system. The second type of knowledge is a weakly cononical part in which that agent's decision space is coupled to one or more decision spaces of other agents. The final component is the hard cononical part. This component is essential to and important in a large number of the other agents. Indeed, in an extreme case all of the agents might overlap in this area of knowledge. The original expert system now can be represented according to the decomposition of the peer agents as the sum of all the weak cononical parts plus the sum of all the cononical parts plus the sum of the hard cononical parts. If there are, for instance, three independent problems, all of the agents are represented simply as cononical knowledge. If there are also weak cononical parts as well as a hard cononical part, the coupling between the agents can be seen as stronger and the conflict resolution burden more difficult.

Benefits of Multiple Agents

There are many benefits to the approach of breaking up a problem into multiple agents. They include control of the development process, modularity, performance, and the ability to maintain, verify, and distribute the solution. The methodologies and the philosophies associated with cooperating expert systems are definitely state of the art in nature. VAX, with its strong orientation toward distributed communications and interprocess communications, firmly supports the development of applications in this format. It should be noted that VMS, the operating system on most VAX computers, usually prefers to have large collections of small processes as opposed to small collections of large processes. That is not to say that a 100-megabyte or even larger process cannot be built on a VAX. It is to say that five 200-megabyte processes are not as desirable as ten 100-megabyte or twenty 50-megabyte ones.

Cooperating expert systems allows the best use of the VAX architecture, software functionality, and resources. It is very much in the philosophy of the VAX architecture and functionality itself. This benefit is particularly important in the development of technology and applications that are in line with what the vendor provides as opposed to stretching to the breaking point the design center that can currently be bought from a salesperson.

The Modes of Operation

The Cooperating Mode

After decoupling the problem along functionality and task lines into a set of agent boundaries, a paradigm in needed that will allow cooperation between these peer processes to arrive at a decision. You can successfully use the following paradigm. It is by no means the only one possible, but it is one that works. The first mode of operation is the cooperating mode. For this mode, if there are any weak cononical parts or hard cononical representation with a given agent, it is necessary to put in a constraint propagation model in a given agent for all the other agents in the system that have any degree of coupling with that agent. Otherwise this step is not necessary. This usually is not the case and more often than not every agent contains constraint probagation models for all the other agents.

In the cooperating mode, expert system A makes a decision FOO. Expert system B relies on that decision to either make a different type of decision or to do some other sort of intelligent processing. Let us say that decision FOO has passed, in A, the constraint probagation model of expert system B. When this decision is given to expert system B, B treats FOO as a constraint that it has to use and tries to make its decision within the context of FOO. In this first mode of operation, we make the assumption that if the decision of expert system A passes through the constraint probagation model of expert system B that is in A, B stands a high probability of being able to make use of that decision to continue intelligent processing. It is obvious that the optimality of A's decision cannot be guaranteed nor can even its total feasibility. This is because of the desire to keep the constraint propagation models small.

If you specified constraint propagation models that always guaranteed feasibility let alone optimality, each of the agents would end up being the equivalent of the single big expert system, which is totally undesirable and where we started. The goal of these constraint propagation models is to be the min/max knowledge segments of all the agents in any agent, the minimum knowledge that gives the maximum information about how the other peer agents function in the overall solution of the problem. The cooperation mode is the fastest mode of conflict resolution between the expert systems. It is the one that is highly desirable and can lead to a seemingly parallel computation environment. Expert system A arrives at the decision FOO, hands it off to expert system B, expert system B arrives at the decision BAR, hands it off to expert system A, and both FOO and BAR pass the appropriate constraint models. Both expert systems A and B continue intelligent processing without a hiccup. This is the most desirable mode of operation.

The Collaboration Mode

The second mode of conflict resolution in cooperating expert systems is called the collaboration mode. Suppose that expert system A arrived at the decision FOO and passed it off to B and even though it passed the min/max constraint probagation model of B in A, the decision FOO is unacceptable for any one of a number of reasons to expert system B. In the collaboration mode, expert system B turns to the peer agent A and enters into a dialogue. It tells A that the decision FOO is either undesirable or unfeasible for its processing function. It recommends to A alternatives that might be better for it and attributes that would characterize a feasible or more optimal decision. With this information, expert system A reevaluates its intelligent reasoning process to come up with a decision FOO2. FOO2 is then handed to expert system B and either this is acceptable or again collaboration is required. The collaboration need not be only in the direction of B to A; it might be from A to B with expert system A saying to B, "Well, this is really the best that I can do — can't you really live with this decision? I know it's not optimal, but it allows me to get a feasible solution as well." The collaboration mode takes longer than the cooperation mode to arrive at a decision, but its use is necessary in order to arrive at an overall solution to the problem.

The Meta Mode

The third mode of operation in a cooperating expert system revolves around building an expert system, in addition to the agents, that essentially functions as the operating system to the application. I call this additional expert system "meta." This mode addresses the fact that when a single large expert system is broken up into a bunch of cooperating agents, an n-person game theoretical situation as opposed to a single-person game theoretical situation is created. (An analogy is that the difference between cooperating expert systems and a single expert system is the difference between a scaler optimization problem and a multiobjective vector optimization problem and to view meta as being the plant general manager and the order entry, scheduling, and production control experts as being the managers of those various departments.)

Each one of the cooperating agents has its own objective function and is trying to perform its intelligent processing to obtain the best result for its objective. When the collaboration mode is initiated between two or more expert agents, meta begins to monitor the process. For instance, it might look at the transactions between the expert systems, monitor queues, or review the status and attributes of the intelligent decision process.

Meta's view of the problem is different from that of the other systems. Rather than worrying about the specifics of a particular segment of the problem, it worries about the overall solution to the problem. The content of its knowledge base has to do with the overall goals and objectives that characterize an intelligent solution to the application. Meta is the grand arbitrator. At one level, it wants to solve and arbitrate the solution to a multiperson nonzero sum optimization problem in which each game player is one of the cooperating agents. The solution that characterizes this problem is usually called the "paretian frontier," or the set of noninferior-nondominated solutions. Meta should steer the solution toward this frontier, when it is described in its knowledge base, as well as toward attributes of how to approach it. If time constraints are critical, meta might simply lay down a mandate to arbitrate the conflict between two or more of the peer agents.

Meta has many functions other than providing the overall supervision to the cooperating expert system. However, this function of grand conflict resolution is central to meta's existence. If the expert system application must perform in a totally autonomous self-contained manner, meta is the ultimate resolver of conflict and must be provided with the type of arbitration knowledge necessary to be able to dictate a solution so that intelligent processing of the agents can continue. Therefore, meta must have a model that represents the possible conflicts that could arise between the agents and that gives the acceptable solutions; a provable finite state knowledge arbitration mechanism must be built inside the knowledge base of meta. If there are no unanticipated conflicts, with provable correctness in a finite state mechanism the solution to the problem can be guaranteed. To the extent that there are unanticipated conflicts, the solution to the problem cannot be guaranteed even though the underlying agents will usually, through the collaboration mode, find some acceptable solution to most problems.

Human Intervention

If the expert system is not a completely and totally autonomous entity, there is a fourth mode of conflict resolution available to the architect and the designer of a cooperating expert system (see Figure 3-3). In this fourth mode, on a selective basis meta would question an enduser in an intelligent fashion. It would present the enduser with the state of processing, the conflict, and the possible alternatives that

- Cooperation
- Collaboration
- Meta
- End User Assistance

Figure 3-3 The different modes in conflict resolution.

are being explored. In this mode the enduser would be allowed to step in and resolve the conflict. This fourth mode of operation is very beneficial in most nonautonomous applications. It is one that guarantees the timely and efficient use of human resources to aid the expert agent environment in the solution to the overall problem.

Tools, Techniques, and Methodologies

There are many possible tools, techniques, and methodologies that can be used in the architecture, design, and implementation of cooperating expert systems. Building state-of-the-art expert systems is not an exact science. It is part science and part art. It usually requires refinement and iteration among the agents and the use of meta in terms of responsibility, functionality, and knowledge. Tuning is necessary to accomplish the overall solution and design goals. First you must find a decomposition strategy to describe the agent's decision space (see Figure 3-4). Next, you must build the appropriate constraint propagation models to allow intelligent cooperation in the first mode of conflict resolution. Then you must build the knowledge interchange mechanism to allow direct communication and arbitration between a subcollection of agents. Meta is a key component in the methodology associated with cooperating expert systems. Care, attention, and detail to what comprises its knowledge and functionality must be given throughout the life cycle of a cooperating expert system application.

Finally, you must be precise about when and how a human user is involved in efficiently resolving conflicts between the agents. It is ab-

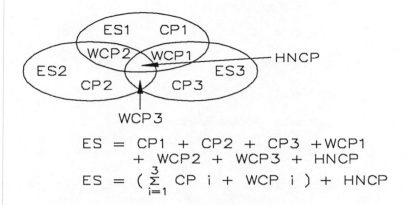

$$ES = CP1 + CP2 + CP3 + WCP1 + WCP2 + WCP3 + HNCP$$

$$ES = \left(\sum_{i=1}^{3} CP\,i + WCP\,i \right) + HNCP$$

● Modes of operation

Automatic
Interactive
Manual override
Guaranteed automatic
Shadowed What If

Figure 3-4 The different modes of utilization.

solutely necessary to develop not only communication protocols between the agents and meta but also knowledge protocols to allow intelligent decision making to proceed. The above paradigm of cooperating expert systems is a higher-order concept than what is normally referred to as a blackboard architecture. A blackboard architecture provides a communication protocol and a knowledge interchange protocol. What it does not specify is what that knowledge means within the context of a particular agent or meta. This aspect is problem specific. Blackboards are not the only technique for arriving at communication and knowledge exchange protocols and interfaces, and again, they are not the answer to specifying the interpretation of that knowledge within the context of overall intelligent problem solution. The burden of that rests firmly on the shoulders of the knowledge engineer.

The Transaction Model

An alternative model that is most useful with VAX is that of the transaction model. I like to cast knowledge interchange and communication in a transaction sense in all of the above modes. Transaction models are much in line with the philosophy of computation of the VAX architecture. In addition, they permit nice characteristics with respect to high availability, recovery, performance, and distribution. It is important to understand that whether a blackboard architecture or a transaction architecture or another possible candidate is used, it does not solve by itself the problem of cooperating expert systems. It provides a foundation for knowledge interface and communication, not for its interpretation within the context of an agent, across agents, or in solution of the overall problem.

Other Techniques

Techniques from operations research and decision theory can be beneficial and useful in casting, solving, and building cooperating expert system environments. Try as much as possible to view these agents as game players in a multiperson game. Try both declaratively and procedurally to maintain very clearly what the objective or objectives are of each agent and in each agent and to maintain the objective or objectives of the overall problem solution to the n-person game theoretical problem in meta. Key to meta's existence is knowledge that will tell meta how to steer or mandate a solution given the current state of the solution, the goals of the underlying agents that are in conflict, and the overall goal of the problem.

Theoretical Tools

There are many tools that greatly benefit the development of cooperating expert systems. Some are highly theoretical and academic in nature. Others are very practical and industrial. A highly theoretical one is the ability to take the single big expert system, run it through a code fragment, and have as the output of that code fragment the appropriate collection of cooperating expert systems. We are long away from a level of understanding and capability to do this, yet this presents a great research opportunity in the further development of AI. Such a tool is not that dissimilar from writing an intelligent compiler that makes use of a truly parallel processing environment. If a software engineer is able to program as if he or she had a uniprocessor and keeps the program simple and lets the compiler figure out the decouplings, the parallelisms, and the arbitration with respect to the underlying machine, in many ways the result is a piece of code that has the technology necessary to solve the cooperating expert system problem. But, we are a long way from the practical use of this technique.

Generic Interfaces and Protocols

More pragmatic tools include developing a generic communication and knowledge interchange interface and protocol. With it, you are closer to being able to quickly and intelligently attack cooperating expert problems. It can be used if you standardize on a blackboard architecture and implement a standard tool to be used over again or if you use the transaction-oriented model and build an intelligent client server paradigm.

A technique in the design of cooperating expert systems is for the knowledge engineer to identify very quickly and efficiently what knowledge and what decisions are really necessary to perform a particular task and piece of functionality and to mark that knowledge as either unique to a particular agent or not. Understanding the decision space of all the agents and what knowledge is necessary to make a decision and what decisions affect other agents is key to the decomposition and tuning of the cooperating expert system.

This orientation is very different from the traditional orientation of a knowledge engineer who has a big expert system model firmly entrenched in his or her mind. Many people have wanted to build cooperating expert systems, yet, when confronted with the problems of conflict resolution across the agents, have decided to build a single model for a single decision space over a single knowledge space. In order to create cooperating expert systems, the knowledge engineer must ask additional questions and have at least an initial decomposition of the problem in mind. That decomposition will need to be refined; for example, a task or piece of functionality might be taken out of one agent and put directly into another to reduce the conflicts that might ensue.

Generic Meta

Another important tool would be to design and implement a relatively flexible and generic meta. Meta is both a technique necessary in cooperating expert systems and a potential software tool. If the definition of meta is broadened from the chairman of the board to the chairman of the board *and* the operating system of the application, you can see very quickly that many services that a specific meta might provide in a specific application would be necessary across many applications. One specific service is obtained because meta is the central service authority and all reference is made to meta. This means that even in the cooperation and collaboration modes A does not know where B is or necessarily its name or specific functionality. All references are made to meta and meta figures out which of the agents need to know this decision or piece of knowledge and appropriately provides the knowledge interface and communication protocol. For reasons of verification, validation, and distribution it is desirable to make all reference to meta rather than to hot wire any paths directly to a particular agent. Other examples of services that meta might provide to the overall environment include access to traditional databases, communications, justification and explanation, reporting, and user interfaces. Definitely, a large component of meta is application or problem specific and can only be specified, designed, and implemented with respect to a particular problem. However, the structure, architecture, and many of the facilities that comprise meta would be needed frequently and can be codified once and used in many cooperating expert systems.

Conclusion

The complexities associated with cooperating expert systems and the four fundamental modes of operations require a shift in philosophy from the traditional knowledge engineering approach. The philosophy encompasses a lot more thought, design, and structuring up front before any implementation, let alone incremental development, ensues. In the big expert system model there is a temptation to start implementing in conjunction with learning how to solve the present problem. This makes more sense because the system is essentially a totally centralized single model whose data, knowledge, control, and logic space are closed and defined over one another. Because this is not the case with cooperating agents, massive iterations of tuning can be needed because of poorly thought out decomposition strategies, constraint probagation models, and conflict arbitration schemes. A good initial design that is well worked out on paper will go a long way toward efficiently implementing a cooperating expert system solution to a problem. This is not to say that there is not a role for incremental development in cooperating expert systems but that a tremendous amount of thought must be given up front to structuring the problem, as well as to addressing the problem so as to minimize the difficulties of conflict resolution across the agents rather than to maximize them.

4

Distributed Artificial Intelligence

To date, most work in the area of AI and expert systems can be characterized as the development of centralized single expert systems that more often than not perform in an advisory capacity. Some people have put these systems directly into a control structure such as a feedback loop in a process plant, attempting to obtain automatic inferencing in the overall solution to the problem. However, most applications are distributed in nature, having many communication protocols and different requirements throughout an organization. They include requirements such as persistence, high availability, survivability, fault tolerance, and the like that make a centralized approach inappropriate in many circumstances.

The requirements that come with building large-scale systems also require consideration. The single-CPU model has limitations, and expert systems and other AI technology approaches are very resource intensive. Only smaller knowledge systems or the use of very, very large and powerful computing environments makes the centralized approach possible. There is a better way, and that way stems from a paradigm of computation that is based on distribution.

The Paradigm

When a large-scale expert problem is viewed as being composed of many pieces along two axes, multiple strategies for distribution can be quickly developed. The first axis might lie along the line of fundamental computer services, and the second might be made up of the components involved in the solution of the application. Networking environments, such as DECnet, provide excellent communication spines upon which to build sophisticated distributed AI systems. Inherently, all of these communication protocols and environments from vendors and particularly from DEC tend to be of a nodal nature as opposed to communication environments in which in the operating system and the communication protocol are truly distributed. However, whether the vendor gives you distribution or gives you nodality, you can still impose a paradigm of computation that allows for the distribution of an AI system.

The Client Server Model

The objective is to obtain a client server model. The model that DECnet presents is nodal. With it, if you have three machines, A, B, C, your model of the network is the union of machines A, B, and C. This granularity is not sufficient for truly distributed AI systems. There are low-level services, however, that can be used appropriately to improve on this.

In a client server paradigm, any computational entity in the configuration can be either a client or a server or both. A client is a particular entity that needs some computation or resource. A server is a particular entity that can provide some computation or resource or some set of computations or resources (see Figure 4-1). If this view is used to develop a piece of software that resides on every computational device in the network, from the software engineering viewpoint the model (i.e., the virtual machine) is not the union of all the nodes but is the union of all the clients plus all the servers. With this view, the granularity can be made even finer if necessary. The virtual machine could become not only the union of all the clients and servers that exist at a given computational instant, but the union of all the clients and servers that exist or could exist in the future.

This virtual machine presents an ideal model from which to build distributed AI systems. The essence of this logic is captured in Figure 4-1. This piece of software, which we will call "meta," makes use of underlying services that are provided by the vendor, such as transparent and nontransparent DECnet and remote tasking. However, it abstracts away the intimate technical details of providing the client

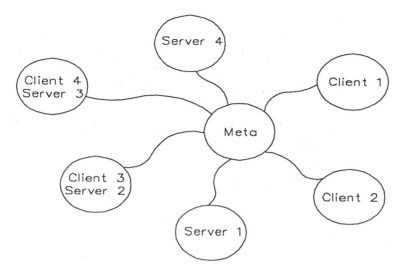

Figure 4-1 Client server model.

server functionality. For this piece of software, it is necessary to build interfaces to the various heuristic environments and IO functions as well as to the traditional computing ones. An example of this would be accessing the paradigm from VAX LISP stream functions so that a given heuristic computational entity could request or return service by simply using symbolic streams. Another example would be providing functionality so that a given inference engine could use the ability to distribute from either the left-hand or the right-hand side of a rule (i.e., calling on a cooperating expert system to do pattern matching or returning a result in the form of a service).

It is in this context that I say that what is needed in distributed AI is a symbolic client server paradigm. What I mean by this is that in the heuristic environments the primitives, functionality, and computational resources are made accessible to the client server paradigm within their context. Figure 4-2 shows examples of symbolic manipulations of a client server paradigm.

It is important to build this client server paradigm on the concept of a transaction model. While a request for a service or the response to a client can be made into a transaction, by making the symbolic client server paradigm transaction based and incorporating some of the key facilities in meta, high availability, persistence, and survivability of the distributed AI application can be accomplished. Figure 4-3 il-

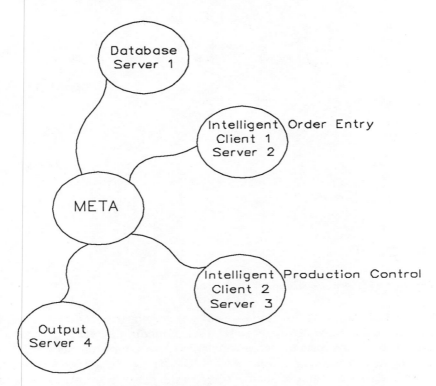

Figure 4-2 Example of use in a heuristic environment.

lustrates examples of the transaction concept for the client server paradigm in a symbolic context.

In addition to the above, the transaction bodies of any given transaction should be objects that are meaningful to heuristic environments. An example of this would be a request for service that is formulated in the transaction body as a recursive list. Being able to ship objects such as lists and structures around the network improves the symbolic nature of the distribution strategy. There are many constructs that can be supported. Different applications will require different symbolic entities as the main body of the transaction.

Meta

Meta was introduced in Chapter 3 in a discussion of cooperating expert systems. There, meta was perceived as the operating system to

```
( TH TB TT )  —  Symbolic  Transaction
  ⌣   |   ⌣
Head  Body  Tail
```

Example:

(Time_Tag Transaction_Type Transaction_Number) = TH

(Foo Bar (Mumble(Mumble))) = TB

(Priority Error_Handling On_Completion) = TT

Figure 4-3 Symbolic transaction.

those cooperating agents. Meta can also have a centralized nature or it can itself be a distributed object. In extending meta to be a distributed object, meta has to be made a self-aware entity, meaning that meta on one machine must be aware of the state and existence of meta on another machine. In the client server paradigm, all references are actually made to meta. A given client or service does not really know where anything is running in the network or know the intimate computer details of how to get at something in a consistent fashion.

Meta is a candidate for tremendous intelligence. It can be given additional logic that encompasses a data-flow model of computation. This model would allow meta to intelligently decide on alternate resources and routing. Meta itself is an ideal candidate for an integrated AI module with a low-level component that provides high performance, traditional communication, and computing functionality and with a higher-level reasoning component that worries about survivability, persistence, resource allocation, and overall efficiency in the environment.

The Implementation Model

In order to accomplish the goal of distributed AI, there is an opportunity to build an intelligent module that implements a symbolic client server paradigm with a data-flow model of computation that is transaction oriented. Moreover, this software model could be built using standard IO and communication facilities that a vendor such as Digital provides but that abstracts away all the intimate technical details. There are other alternatives to this model and paradigm for distributed AI, such as a blackboard architecture.

The terms blackboards and blackboard architecture are often used as synonyms for ways to provide cooperating expert systems and to solve its problems. They should not be. Chapter 3 clearly details a paradigm and a philosophy of computation to address cooperating expert systems and shows that a key problem is the conflict resolution across the pier agents. In order to allow the agents to resolve their conflicts, there obviously need to be communication paths that provide knowledge interfaces and knowledge exchange mechanisms. The blackboard architecture is an alternative structure to a transaction processing model of a client server nature, and transaction-based systems that are symbolic in nature and intelligent are more desirable. This is because of the persistent nature of transaction systems. In the real world, there are many requirements to fill, such as survivability in the face of something going wrong with the hardware. A transaction model will better serve these requirements. In terms of providing the knowledge interface and communication requirements between peer agents none of the necessary and desirable attributes are lost by this approach.

The computation philosophy of distributed AI is a totally synergistic concept with cooperating expert systems. These two philosophies feed and support each other. For example, if you build a single big expert system that is designed to execute in a single process, you have limited the entities that you can distribute. The finer your cooperating expert system rationale, the more distributed the application is. Likewise, the paradigm of a symbolic client server model with a data-flow computational structure based on transaction processing only requires one CPU in the virtual machine topology. Whether you have one machine or twenty machines, the software engineering model is exactly the same; nothing changes. This is very important to understand because it means that if you architect, design, and build your systems this way, you essentially can deliver on a whole host of configurations.

Benefits of the Approach

The benefits of this approach are many. First, by relaxing the single-CPU model, integrated AI systems can be built that have a high degree of availability in case of failure. In many industries it is unacceptable for the application to be unavailable if a disk or a computer fails. Only through the use of distributed AI can these requirements can be met.

In addition, distributed AI is exceedingly compute intensive. It is important to be able to decompose a problem and to use the most cost-effective computing environments possible to address it. With Digital equipment, by having a meta that provides the client server paradigm with the data-flow model of computation in a transaction format, you have the choice of delivering five MicroVAX IIs or a single 8650. This is important to understand. Your system, if designed from this viewpoint, can act like a rubber band. You can build systems as large or as small as you want. From the viewpoint of software engineering, the code does not change.

The ability to effectively use many computers rests upon having computational entities that can be distributed. First, if the application is broken into cooperating expert systems, there should be a collection of peer modules that can be distributed. In most problems, it should be very easy to find at least three, if not four or five, obvious candidates for cooperating expert systems. If an intelligent CIM system is used as an example, the following candidates for intelligent cooperation can be easily identified.

- Computer-aided instruction
- Alarm management
- Scheduling
- Maintenance
- Statistical process control
- Process modeling
- Control
- Simulation
- Plant planner and optimizer
- Order entry
- Inventory
- Decision support

Usually, when building an application, you should not deal at first with all these aspects. However, within the design center of a particular project or product, you will usually find more than a couple of logical candidates for distribution. A second idea is to look at the fundamental computer resources that are needed — for instance, the database component, number crunching, the graphics user interface, and special-purpose output. An application can have an arbitrary collection of VAXs: database machines running Rdb, number crunching machines running Fortran and C numerical algorithms, knowledge-base machines doing symbolic computation such as inferencing, and graphics workstations in which the intelligent user interface and natural language processing takes place. When looking at a given problem, it is easy to find a strategy for distributing the problem. Given the CPU-intensive nature of AI, you should set a firm foundation so that you do not run into problems as the requirements of the application grow.

This approach also relaxes the constraints that all heuristic programming environments tend to have. Some of these constraints are in the areas of stable storage, computational efficiency, ability to be integrated, and the like. The transaction-based symbolic client server paradigm with a data-flow model of computation can provide stable storage to the heuristic environments to intelligently access traditional databases. In addition, they provide a symbolic transaction integration path between any one thing and another. This is a very important point. If a problem is cast along these communication and knowledge interface lines, anything can be integrated with anything else on the VAX: OPS5 to LISP, LISP to ART, ART to Rdb, Rdb to NEXPERT Object, NEXPERT Object to LISP. Nothing is left out as a candidate for meaningful integration in the solution of a problem. In addition, the distribution helps to provide high-performance solutions to time-critical problems. It becomes natural, easy, and desirable to be able to throw cost-effective computations against computation-intensive problems.

When confronted with developing a state-of-the-art expert system for a given application, it is very easy to get caught up in the physics of the domain and the philosophy of rapid prototyping. This enthusiasm to get logic up and running and demonstrable most often leads to unwieldy systems that are highly oriented toward small knowledge structures as opposed to large-scale expert systems. If you keep the philosophies of distributed AI, cooperating expert systems, and integrated AI clear, you will be better served throughout the life cycle of the project and the product.

Synergy with Cooperating Expert Systems

Over the years I have seen many instances in which architectural and design opportunities were ignored and later on the entire system had to be rewritten in order to deliver a production system. Given the synergy between cooperating expert systems and distributed AI, the solution and the application should be modeled along these philosophies from the beginning. This will result in a solution architecture that is highly maintainable, highly performance oriented, easily extended, and very naturally delivered in a production sense to varying and different real-world environments. If the synergy of distributed AI with cooperating expert systems is totally forgotten, the ability to distribute is greatly limited if the system is not rewritten for deployment. Cooperating expert systems, distributed AI, and integrated AI begin to form a philosophy of computation that is in line with delivering real-world AI applications. Architects, designers, and technical managers need to be aware of these aspects in order to deliver a system that fulfills present and future requirements easily on a cost-effective basis.

Tools, Techniques, and Methodologies

There are many tools, techniques, and methodologies that are necessary for distributed AI. One tool is obvious. That is the existence of a meta that runs on every computer in the configuration and provides the paradigm of a symbolic client server model with a data-flow computational structure and a transaction-processing underpinning. This tool can be made as intelligent or as bare bones as desired. At the lower levels of this tool, traditional programming environments such as C can be easily used to provide the fundamental transaction processing and communication primitives. On top of this layer inference- and noninference-based symbolic environments can be used to obtain as high a degree of intelligence as desired. An example of a high degree of intelligence has to do with load balancing, performance, tuning, and monitoring.

Meta can decide where the agents run in the configuration. For the moment, let us say that there are three cooperating expert systems, a traditional database, and a number crunching environment. And let us say there are three computers, A, B, and C. Meta, by being able to reason about transactions loads, queues, arrival times, service times, and resource use and status of the three machines, can intelligently decide where any module should be executing at any time. As indicated earlier, meta is an ideal candidate for an integrated AI expert system in its own right.

There are a number of techniques that you should be aware of when using distributed AI. The first technique is that of integrated AI, being able to combine traditional computing with heuristic computing. Meta will require this as well as the overall philosophy of computation. The second technique is that of cooperating expert systems. Since many of the modules that will be distributed in this AI environment are of a heuristic nature, it will be important for meta to be able to handle the conflict resolution across peer agents. In addition, meta must be able to be a self-aware process and to arbitrate conflicts between peer metas. The levels of conflict resolution discussed in Chapter 3 need to be supported by meta. In addition, a flexible interface must be developed that will allow the easy configuration of meta for different run-time network topologies and will also configure what the underlying clients and servers are.

Methodologically speaking, you need to look at the application and for every computational entity decide what can be a client and what can be a server at any point. All references should be made to meta. Meta knows the intimate technical details of coercion into environments that are seemingly disparate and can find out where any computational entity lives. The burdens should be put on meta and the general distributed AI and cooperating expert system environment and not on the underlying clients and servers themselves. It is important to have a methodology for determining a distribution philosophy. Basically, take the graphics user interface, natural language processing, and anything else to do with the user and put it on graphics workstations such as the VAX station. Then view the VAXs, whether they are MicroVAX IIs or 8800s, as specific entities of computation such as database, communications, knowledge-base, or number crunching machines. Meta can change the roles of a given machine at any time or augment those roles based upon its logic of load balancing, performance, tuning, and monitoring. This view of distribution based on the two fundamental axes that were indicated earlier is central to the philosophy.

In addition, meta must be able to support any fundamental modes that the system needs to be in. One mode is the production computational state in which the live solution of the problem takes place. Another is an experimental state that allows what-if scenarios to be played with given the underlying expert application in a nondestructive fashion. There are also the modes of automatic pilot, human interaction, and direct manual overrides for any fundamental modes that are anticipated.

Conclusion

Distributed AI is totally in line with the real-world environments that exist in both the industrial and commercial sectors today. By building a few tools, by developing some standard corporate techniques and methodologies, and by using this philosophy along with cooperating expert systems and integrated AI, you will set a firm foundation for many years to come. Digital provides excellent substraight tools and environments on which to build distributed AI systems. By using the facilities in DECnet, in their cluster technology and wide area and local area offerings, you can naturally synthesize a meta that will perform the services and functionality described in this chapter.

5

Time-Critical Artificial Intelligence

Time-Critical AI and Expert System Environments

Discussions about time-critical AI are often heated because many people are confused about what time-critical AI is and how to go about addressing it and also because of the difficult reality of a real-world implementation to solve today's time-critical problems with today's expert systems.

There really is only one definition of time criticalness. It is based on finding the time constants of the underlying dynamic system. You must find some sort of dynamic model to represent the state transitions of your system throughout time. In the process world this usually results in a set of simultaneous differential equations, the solution of which results in time constants of the underlying modes of response for the transient response of the system. A fifth-order system will have five time constants; an nth order system will have n time constants. Some people believe that there are truly batch-oriented offline static systems that do not have any dynamics associated with them. This is not true. Every system has dynamics; the only question is the value of the time constants.

All systems are comprised of their transient plus steady state response characteristics. It is the transient response that is of key concern in time-critical AI. After arriving at an elementary or highly complex representation of the dynamics of the system and finding the underlying time constants for all of the modes of the system, you can intelligently talk about time criticalness. Different decisions affect different modes of the transient response. In general, a good rule of thumb to follow is that if you are reasoning about a particular decision that is affected by time constants A, B, and C or that affects those time constants, you can keep control of the system and be timely if you can make the appropriate decision in under one time constant of the smallest of those involved and have all transient responses reach steady state after roughly five time constants. Essentially, the response is quick enough if it comes very early in the transient response curve of the underlying dynamic system. This very simple yet key insight into dynamics leads to a strategy for implementing time-critical expert systems.

The Paradigm

In order to address a problem in which time criticalness is of importance, you must come up with a model that clearly tracks the evolution of the time constants of the underlying system. A typical way to do this is to develop a state space model in which the state variables are not the process physics variables but rather are the time constants themselves. In time-critical expert systems we are not only interested in the evolution of process variables but are very interested in the evolution of the underlying time constants that provide us the constraints under which we must reason. This is where to begin building a time-constraint propagation model in knowledge-based code.

There is a fundamental question that needs to be addressed and that should be understood to appropriately attack a time-critical expert application: How intelligent can you afford to be? The answer to this is very simple. You can afford to be as intelligent as the underlying time-constant constraints allow you to be. For example, if you are reasoning about a particular type of decision and you have arrived at a feasible strategy in under one time constant of the critical mode of the system, you can afford to continue to reason, to search for optimality until you hit the hard time constraint. What this little heuristic statement implies is that in time-critical AI you must set up your search strategies so that you guarantee a feasible decision consistent with the time-constant constraint propagation model and can spend any time that you have left over searching for optimality. This technique works very well and leads to systems that can focus their resources and logical inferences in a directed fashion.

Basically, problems are attacked with AI and expert system technology when a closed-form analytic solution cannot be found. More often than not, search is a key component to arriving at a decision based on knowledge-inference technology. The key questions to time-critical AI are How much time do you have to search? and What should your search strategy be? The answer to the first question lies in the time-constraint propagation model of the underlying dynamic time constants of the system that are manifested in the design and implementation of the expert system application. The search strategy manifests itself as architecting a search method that will spend its energies first guaranteeing feasibility within the time constraints and then searching for as optimal an answer as time will permit. This bifurcation of search strategies more often than not is quite necessary to accomplish the goals of being timely, yet being as intelligent as you can afford to be.

Time-critical constraint-based reasoning with flexible and adaptive search strategies based upon the evolution of the underlying modes of response of the dynamics of the system is a critical architectural, design, and implementation methodology that can be used to address many tough real-time applications that stem from many industries. Unless this issue is specifically attacked with declarative modeling in the knowledge base and procedural representation and inferences in the logic base, it is hard to satisfy the system requirements let alone to optimize for the time that is available.

A common misconception is that if a problem moves more slowly, it is easier to meet the time constraints. Unfortunately, this is only half of the issue being addressed. The other half is how complex the decision-making process is. For example, if you have a 30-second-response-time problem that requires a thousand complex inferences as opposed to a problem in which you have an hour to respond but that requires a million complex inferences, you might be far better off attacking the faster-moving, less complicated problem. This is a fundamental trap that developers and application engineers frequently fall into. They believe that small time constants represent harder time-critical problems than do large time constants. In the development of time-critical AI systems, the underlying time constants of a problem must be compared with the computation burden required in the inferencing to get a true reading of how difficult a time-critical application is.

The Implementation

In the implementation of time-critical expert systems there are other synergistic methodologies and philosophies that will result in an overall responsive system. The techniques of integrated AI, cooperating expert systems, and distributed AI provide meaningful contributions to responsiveness in any vendor's platform. For example, if part of any application requires the inversion of a 1000 by 1000 matrix, it is much better to do it in Bliss, Fortran, or C than in LISP or in some other inferential symbolic environment. On the VAX using the right tool for the right piece of the problem aids in solving time-critical inferential-based problems.

With cooperating expert systems, the problem can be broken up and made more manageable, and the resource can be better allocated on the particular computer. This also provides a platform on which to intelligently reason about time criticalness in the expert system itself. Finally, with distributed AI, the single-CPU model can be relaxed and as much computing power as is required can be brought in, given the associated cost constraints of the problem solution. Using the model of time-critical constraint propagation to arrive at a directed bifurcating search strategy and combining it with the architectural methodologies of integrated AI, cooperating expert systems, and distributed AI will give you an excellent platform on which to tune the implementation to meet the requirements of responsiveness along most reasonable dimensions.

An Example

A simple example of the concepts of time-critical AI in a time-critical planning problem with refinement follows (see Figure 5-1):

1. Expert system 1, used for mission planning and flight control, can make decisions in the set D-hat and has underlying time constants in the set tau-hat.
2. The set of decisions D-hat is given by D_1 and D_2.
3. The set of underlying time constants tau-hat is given by tau_1 and tau_2.
4. Tau_1 is equal to a function F_1 of T that is equal to mode 1 of the system and is equal to a constant tau_1.

TIME CRITICAL AI EXAMPLE

$\hat{D}$ = $\{D_1, D_2\}$ Set of decisions

$\hat{\tau}$ = $\{\tau_1, \tau_2\}$ Set of modes or time constants

τ_1 = $S_1(t)$ = mode 1 = τ_1 a constant

τ_2 = $S_2(t)$ = mode 2 = τ_2 a constant

$\tau_1 < \tau_2$

D_1 effects mode 2 $\Longrightarrow$

$T(D_1) < \tau_2$

D_2 effects modes 1 & 2 $\Longrightarrow$

$T(D_2) < \tau_1$

Figure 5-1 An example of time-critical AI.

5. Tau2 is equal to a function F2 of T that equals mode 2 of the system and is equal to the constant tau2.
6. Tau1 is less than tau2.
7. D1 affects mode 2; this implies that the time to make decision D1, T of D1, must be less than tau2.
8. D2 affects modes 1 and 2; this implies that the time to make decision D2, T of D2, must be less than tau1.

Figure 5-2 looks at the search strategies involved. Suppose that we use a hypothetical reasoning format built around a directed acyclic graph (DAG). The hypothetical root of the DAG, as indicated in Figure 5-2, is given by state S1 of the system. We want to make decision D2. The time-constraint propagation model says that we must do this in under tau1 time, and the present time is T1. In this stage of the problem, our search strategy is a directed knowledge-focused strategy that is looking for feasibility. We assume a beam-search strategy, focusing knowledge to direct the beam of width 1.

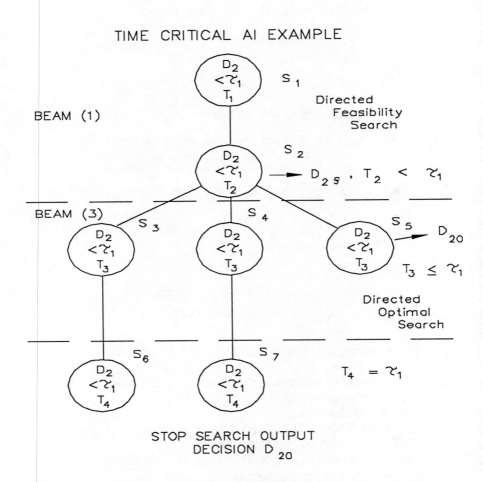

Figure 5-2 The evolution of the time-critical decision component systems.

A new state is generated by S_2. We are still looking for decision D_2, we must propagate the time constraint, and therefore we must still do this under tau_1, and the time is T_2. Let us say that we find such a decision in state 2; this is decision D_{2f}. Time T_2 is less than tau_1. Therefore, we have a feasible solution. Since time is less than the propagated time constraint of the underlying time constant of concern, we switch our search strategy to a knowledge-focused directed optimal search strategy and widen the beam to width 3.

We have three new hypothetical states; S_3, S_4, and S_5. In S_3 we are still looking for a decision D_2, now an alternative optimal candidate. We still have the propagated time constraint of less than tau_1, and we are now at time T_3. In S_4 we are looking for an optimal candidate D_2 in under tau_1, and time is T_3. In S_5 we are looking for a candidate optimal D_2 in under tau_1, and time is T_3. In state 5 we find an optimal candidate, D_{20}. Since time T_3 is less than or equal to tau_1, this is marked as an optimal candidate.

We now continue the directed knowledge-intensive optimal search strategy and generate states of hypothetical decision reasoning S_6 and S_7. However, since T_4 is equal to tau_1, the propagated time constraint, we stop the process and output our optimal decision D_{20}.

This basic sequence of events represents some of the concepts associated with time-critical systems, using a mission planning and flight control application as an example. Directed knowledge-intensive search as opposed to random search is a key aspect of the paradigm of reasoning in time-critical problems.

Benefits of the Approach

The above represents a state-of-the-art paradigm of computation; its benefits are numerous. There is never an infinite amount of computation available, particularly when AI and expert systems are being used in actual industrial and commercial environments. Unless these advanced computational facilities can be intelligently introduced in an efficient manner, the computation demand can be insatiable. With the above paradigm and methodology, a heuristic environment that is tunable and regulated to the demands of the problem can be built. By producing a time-critical solution that is easily extended and modified as computation environments become more efficient, feasible and subsequently optimal answers can be reliably produced on traditional architectures. In addition, a uniform philosophy and model of computation to address these types of problems can be presented.

There are many time-critical applications; they are in the process and financial industries, government systems, and MIS, to name a few. For most of these domains, the delivery vehicle must be on a traditional architecture. Therefore, a new environment must be developed that can be easily tuned so that it can perform within the underlying time constraints. With the above paradigm of reasoning, you can decide how intelligent the system can afford to be and should be and how it goes about focusing its attention to produce that intelligence. Since the paradigm supports multiple bifurcating search strategies that are knowledge intensive and knowledge driven, it gives you heuristic latitudes to focus the expert system in a timely fashion. This focus of attention on where reasoning ensues and how much of the knowledge base need be considered is key to producing high-performance results.

To repeat one of my maxims: Thou shalt develop on what thy will deliver on. By using this paradigm you can avoid the problem of finding out that the prototype is incapable of being delivered in a production environment because it is too slow. Timeliness is addressed explicitly, as opposed to implicitly, with architecture, design, and implementation support that allows incremental refinement as a production environment is approached.

Tools, Techniques, and Methodologies

Getting Started

Many tools, techniques, and methodologies are necessary to accomplish the above. The first step is to build a representation of the underlying evolution of the dynamics and time constants of the system as it relates to the application. This can be done by using a state space model of the underlying time constants in which the components of the state vector are the time constants of the underlying system instead of process variables as normally would be found. There are many other possible ways of modeling the evolution of the time constants. The important thing is to have such a model.

The next step is to analyze the decision space of the expert application and produce a mapping from the set of all possible decisions into the class group of affected time constants in order to find the truly constraining time constant for the fastest moving mode that is affected by that decision. Additionally, an explicit time-constraint propagation model and a supervisory search structure that intelligently can at least strive for feasibility must be built in the inference engine. Then you should bifurcate and look for optimality. Additionally, it is important in the development of these multiple search strategies that address time-critical problems to include knowledge that will allow the system to intelligently meet the exogenous and indigenous needs of the application and search strategies. It is very important to be able to cut down search as much as possible and to be able to make the search strategies more efficient as more is known about the problem. This is the difference from simply conducting a blind search in which no rationale is known.

In the earlier example, the width of the beam and the modes that are chosen for exploration were knowledge directed and knowledge intensive. The beam width was not arbitrary nor were the exploration choices for states evaluated randomly. Incorporating knowledge methodologies and knowledge directedness in the framework can dramatically improve time-critical responsiveness.

Combining Methodologies

Another important methodology and technique to employ in developing time-critical systems is that of integrated AI. In producing time-critical and highly responsive expert systems, it is important to use the most computationally efficient resource and paradigm that does not prohibitively delay development time. This means that if a fast fourier transform has to be performed so that the result can be used for inferencing to decide what next needs to be done, the transform is implemented in a highly efficient numerical language, such as Fortran, and not in LISP or OPS. This seemingly obvious statement is very important in traditional architectures. You pay a price for data-driven computation and symbolic flexibility. In order to produce efficient solutions to complicated and difficult time-critical problems, disparate computing environments must be blended together. Cooperating expert systems and distributed AI are also part of the techniques and methodologies used to accomplish time criticalness.

With cooperating expert systems, the problem can be broken up into more efficient intelligent computational modules. Therefore, instead of having one very large pattern and join net that must always be active, you can have a large collection of smaller pattern and join nets of which only a subset might be active at time. As the data-driven computational environments grow, their performance decreases. Cooperating expert systems leads to more performance-oriented overall results.

Distributed AI can be very critical because it permits the single-CPU model to be relaxed, and it effectively puts more computation into the solution. Suppose you have a time-critical application such as factory automation and no matter how intelligent an implementation of a time-critical paradigm you use, the largest uniprocessor available is insufficient to keep up with the problem. Being able to distribute the problem and increase the amount of computation will give a high degree of confidence that cost might become the ultimate consideration, not the feasibility of solving the problem on a traditional architecture such as the VAX.

Conclusion

Time-critical AI, distributed AI, cooperating expert systems, and integrated AI are all synergistic technologies. They feed each other, they reinforce each other, and they make the sum much greater than the individual parts.

6

Domain-Dependent
Solution Shells

The Paradigm

Much of the bristling activity to date in the area of expert systems and
knowledge bases has been of the one-shot unreusable type. For example, in the process industries there is a particular problem such as
alarm management. An expert system is built that is good for the particular process under consideration in a particular plant. This approach leads to a highly specific inflexible solution. An alternative approach is the domain-dependent solution shell.

It is commonly recognized that the term "shell" refers to a
knowledge engineering or expert programming environment that
provides general paradigms of artificial intelligence reasoning. These
environments are usually called shells because their paradigms of
computation are layered on top of some other substraight computing
environment such as LISP or C. Examples of the commonly found
domain-*independent* shells would be OPS5 by Digital Equipment Corporation, ART the automated reasoning tool by Inference Corporation,
KEE by Intellicorp, NEXPERT Object by Neuron Data, S1 by
Teknowledge, and Knowledge Craft by the Carnegie Group. The
domain-independent shells are not particularly suited or ill suited for
any class of problem. Depending on your point of view, they are equal-

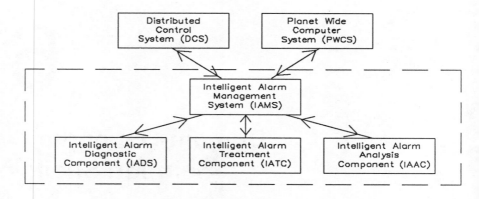

Figure 6-1 Intelligent alarm management system.

ly applicable or inapplicable to problems in the process industries, computer integrated manufacturing, finance, MIS/DP, government systems, etc.

A domain-dependent solution shell can be thought of as a domain-specific solution shell. The concept here is one of specific functionality to a specific problem in a specific domain whereby the shell allows a class group of problems to be easily addressed without deep artificial intelligence or computer science knowledge on the part of the user. Putting your time and energies into the construction of a domain-specific solution shell will result in much greater leverage for a vendor or end user.

An Example

As an example, let us turn back to alarm management (see Figure 6-1). In alarm management, there is a situation in which either no alarms are going off in a particular plant or many alarms are being signaled. These alarms are related to process variables as well as to control variables in the manufacturing environment. Instead of continually building from scratch an expert system that can diagnose what the real problem is when a number of alarms are signaled, it would be better to build a flexible environment that could handle a wide number of specific alarm management situations.

An intelligent alarm management system would be comprised of three fundamental capabilities. The first is the diagnostic component. This part of the knowledge base would answer the following question: Given that a number of alarms have been signaled, what is actually causing the problem? More often than not, this is not obvious in a real plant environment. The second component of such a system would be the treatment component. Given that you know what is causing the problem, what should be done about it? The third and final component of an intelligent alarm management system would be the analysis component. This component attempts to monitor the results and reasoning of both the diagnostic and treatment components to infer how to more intelligently process situations. It is this component that manifests the logic of learning with respect to sensitivity analysis in such entities as alarm-level thresholds.

Domain-specific shells use a number of tools, both traditional and heuristic in nature, including a domain-independent shell such as OPS or ART, to provide an environment that thinks and communicates in terms of the physics of alarm management in the process industries. The shell in our example, although flexible, can only be used to solve alarm management problems. It is specific to the alarm management physics. It is comprised of primitives, functionality, and syntax that make sense in the context of alarm management and is nonsense with respect to anything else. Ideally, such a domain-dependent shell should require no computer science or programming to use it. When the shell shows up at a particular site, it will be incapable of performing any productive work at first. A necessary first step would be to make the shell specific to a particular plant situation.

Site-Specific Knowledge Acquisition

This first step is the site-specific knowledge acquisition phase (see Figure 6-2). In this phase the shell needs to be taught in a simple manner the site-specific configuration, goals, objectives, rules, and integration paths as well as anything — operational or procedural information — that is necessary to solve the particular problem at that particular site. This knowledge acquisition phase is accomplished through the use of form systems, graphically oriented knowledge-base

```
Plant Object  _____

Process Name  _____

Inputs  _____

Outputs  _____

Control Points  _____

Alarm Points  _____

Control Goals  _____

Alarm Threshholds  _____

Corrective Actions  _____

        Plant Object Form
```

Figure 6-2   Example form in a knowledge acquisition system for a domain-specific solution shell.

editors, natural-language processors, and other mechanisms that simplify and abstract away any and all computer science or artificial intelligence details.

Levels of Shell Use

At its height, one might view a domain-dependent solution shell as an integrated artificial intelligence application with the flexibility to solve a broad range of particular problems in a particular vertical market. There are many possibilities for domain-dependent solution shells. Possibilities span the breadth and depth of industries.

If we look at the process industries as an example, we see that there are two levels at which a domain-specific solution shell can be built. The higher level is a shell that provides broad-based functionality. Such high-level shells are shells that are oriented toward solving the control, simulation, estimation, and training problems in a plant environment. At the lower level, there are opportunities for domain-dependent solution shells that address specific problem classes. Such

Figure 6-3 Shell continuum.

problem classes are alarm management, tuning, scheduling, maintenance, process modeling, plant optimization and planning, statical quality control, and the like. Whichever level you address, the key part of the paradigm to focus on is the ease and simplicity of actually applying that shell to a particular real-world problem. As long as this aspect is not lost sight of, you will have a successful endeavor. If, however, you choose a level of abstraction that is sufficiently high, your solution may begin to look more like the domain-independent shells than the domain-specific shells.

You can view the opportunities to provide intelligent shells as being represented on a continual line that has at its origin the domain-independent solution shell, a shell that can be equally applied to almost any problem and that requires a great deal of computer science and artificial intelligence knowledge to make it specific (see Figure 6-3). Further out on this continual line is the higher-level function domain-dependent shells. Such an example might be a shell that solves or is oriented to control problems. Here the shell would provide many primitives and paradigms of reasoning in a default sense to make its application in control situations easier. However, more often than not it will require some level of artificial intelligence and computer science by the user to solve a particular problem. Further out to the right is the true domain-dependent solution shell, an example of which would be a shell that would handle intelligent alarm management in process plants. This shell should require no computer science and artificial intelligence to be made specific to actually solve a particular problem. Finally, the furthest point out on the right is the specific knowledge base that can solve a real problem. What you can see from this continuum is that you could end up with the specific knowledge base by starting at any point on the continuum line. The real question is, How much reusable code will be left after the site-specific knowledge base is completed? It is the domain-specific solution shell concept and paradigm that generates the maximum amount of leverage to any vendor or end-user corporation.

To view the paradigm correctly, you could envision a domain-dependent solution shell as showing up at a site with schemas in the declarative component of the knowledge base, clearly defined at the higher part of a taxonomy and loosely defined at the lower part of a taxonomy. You could envision rules in the procedural component of the knowledge base as either cast in iron and complete or as being of a parametric nature, waiting for specific knowledge to be entered into the declarative component to make them functional and specific. It is through the intelligent knowledge-acquisition site-specific process that the declarative and procedural components of the knowledge base are made specific to the particular situation. The use of intelligent form systems, graphically oriented knowledge-base editors, and natural-language-oriented question and answer sessions are all oriented toward completing both the declarative and the procedural component of the knowledge base to allow intelligent reasoning to ensue at a particular plant.

Benefits of the Approach

Efficient Allocation of Resources

The benefits of the approach of building domain-dependent solution shells are many. First, there is the issue of efficient allocation of resources. Expert systems development is a very expensive and time-consuming endeavor. People, equipment, and software tend to be more costly than do pure traditional-application-oriented problems. If you are going to attack a particular problem such as scheduling, it is highly desirable to do it in such a way that leverage and reusability can be obtained.

Reusability

A second issue stems from the complexities and difficulties in getting anything right. It is not a trivial exercise to build a correct expert-system-based application. The levels of effort and the complexities in computer science and artificial intelligence are severe. If you have ten plants that all need an intelligent alarm management system, it is much better to have one project leading to one piece of code to install in those ten plants than to have ten projects. Even though it is somewhat more difficult to build a correct domain-dependent solution shell than a one-shot expert, overall it turns out to be easier to get it right once as opposed to getting it right ten times. This is a very important point if you are going to deploy significant amounts of expert system and artificial intelligence technology.

Broad Problem Solution

This leads to the third benefit of this approach, which is that by and large the world is really not interested in great computer science and artificial intelligence tools; the world is really interested in solving problems. The closer you are to solving a problem, the greater the receptivity on the part of most organizations. This is true for both the vendor and the end user. In the case of the vendor, you are confronted with the high cost of AI technology and the associated equipment and people to apply it. When you spend your energies developing a great domain-independent solution shell, you are confronted with getting end users to agree to the great costs and associated technical risks of this type of embryonic technology. From the viewpoint of the end user, you find quite often a similar situation. Most end users have computer science and applications engineering groups of their own. These groups might be viewed as internal vendors of solutions and technology to the rest of the corporation. They too are best served by having a domain-dependent solution shell with which to attack a particular class group of problems rather than approaching the plants that would be their customers with more basic technology. If artificial intelligence and expert systems are going to become a wide-spread and massive commercial reality, by and large the approach of domain-dependent solution shells will be needed. Growth is limited if this approach is not taken.

Increased Chances of Success

An additional benefit to this approach is that it broadens the perspective and knowledge engineering of a vendor or end user right up front through the attempt to address a wider class of instances in the real world. All too often when a specific one-shot knowledge base is built, there is the feeling that an expert must be found in a plant. Then this plant and this expert are used in a sort of God-like fashion to architect, design, and implement the knowledge base. Obviously, this approach would not lead to success in constructing a domain-specific solution shell. However, even if the goal is simply to build a specific knowledge base for a specific plant for a specific process, by taking in spirit, if not in deed, the approach of the domain-specific shell, there is a higher probability of success.

This observation stems from the fact that what is needed, even in the one-shot expert system approach, is flexibility. Things in the plant environment, as well as in any other example industry that you might choose, such as finance, are not static. The knowledge base has to be evolved, usually to have some meaningful life expectancy. Moreover, although you usually can find an individual who is recognized as being expert, that individual is not always the quintessential representative of how the problem should be solved. You will find more often than not that there are differences of opinions and techniques even in developing a solution to a one-shot approach. All too often, the one-shot approach based on purely incremental development methodologies leads to a very inflexible capability that is not easy to change or to evolve over time.

The spirit of a domain-dependent solution shell is one of great flexibility and evolution. By design, it takes into account the logic associated with many plants, as well as many experts. This concept is very important to understand. Moreover, if you are going to limit your activities to a specific site with no goal of having reusable and leveragible software in and of itself, it still warrants adhering to the spirit and some of the techniques associated with building a domain-specific shell. Your overall result and probability of success will be much higher.

Tools, Techniques, and Methodologies

Identifying and Representing Knowledge

A number of tools, techniques, and methodologies are associated with the architecture, design, and implementation of a domain-dependent

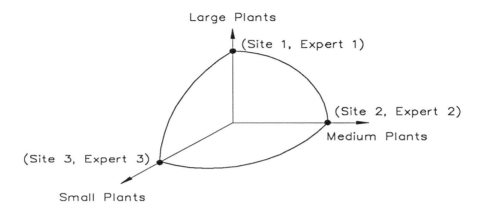

Figure 6-4 Orthogonal decomposition of sites and domain experts to build a domain-specific solution shell.

solution shell. One of the most important methodologies in this area of artificial intelligence is identifying and representing the knowledge associated with a set of domain-experts and sites (see Figure 6-4). As indicated earlier, in the traditional approach of developing a one-shot expert system, one or more knowledge engineers usually interact strongly with a domain expert and a site. Incremental development then ensues until a small knowledge system is arrived at that is deployable to solve the task at hand. In constructing a domain-de-pendent solution shell, this process will not lead to success. Let us take a problem such as alarm management. What is necessary is to find a collection of sites and a collection of domain experts to work with that represent the general problem. All sites are not unequal or equal. This statement also holds true for domain experts. Certain principals, structures, and methods of reasoning are common and others are site-specific. Initially, it is important to interview a rather large number of sites and experts at a superficial level to understand the breath and depth of the problem.

From this initial interviewing process, you then have to make an in-itial decision as to where you are going to draw the line on the boun-daries of what the domain-specific shell can solve. Once this boundary is arrived at, you then need to choose a set of sites and a set of domain experts to work with. Ideally, this set of sites and domain experts should be as orthogonal to each other as possible. You are looking to find the minimum number of sites and experts that gives the maximum span of knowledge that the domain-dependent solution shell will require to be general.

An illustration of the concept is as follows: To solve a particular class of problems in a domain-dependent solution shell format, you must work with three particular plants and three particular domain experts. The plants are representative of the very large, the middle-sized, and the small plant. This is very important because in architecting, designing, and implementing the shell, you need to identify what is common across sites and contrast that with what is different across them. The things that are common can be implemented so that they have a very high performance implementation and are a default part of the system; those aspects that are different can be left in a parametric form that can be acquired through the intelligent knowledge acquisition process. This methodology of finding and working with a set of pseudo-orthogonal sites and domain experts very early on in the architecture, design, and implementation of the domain-specific solution shell is central and critical to its success.

Structuring the Knowledge Base

A key methodology for developing a domain-specific solution shell is the proper structuring of the knowledge base. One-shot expert systems tend to have a loose collection of schemas in the declarative component and a loose collection of rules in the procedural component to perform the intelligent reasoning. This is totally inappropriate for a domain-specific solution shell. It is important to analyze your problem in great detail and to represent your declarative knowledge as knowledge classes. These classes represent aggregates or clusters of schemas that are necessary to model so that they represent the solution of the problem. An example knowledge class would be the site-specific knowledge class. The site-specific configuration, goals, objectives, data structures, and heuristics would be put in this knowledge class. An example from a domain-specific shell for the process industries that does intelligent parametric optimization of distributed control systems would be a knowledge class that models all the tuning optimization methods.

An expert system is not a random firing of rules. It contains an algorithm that leads to a solution. This algorithm is not in closed form analytic solution format, but it does exist. Because of this fact, scheduling in the procedural component in the knowledge base becomes important. The above provides motivation for organizing your collection of rules into rule sets. These rule sets might be maintained in almost a scientific subroutine library format. Because of this, you not only can perform conflict resolution with respect to any rules that are presently on the agenda, but you can perform conflict resolution with respect to any rule sets that are candidates for execution. Organizing the procedural component of the logic base as collections of rule sets that can be scheduled appropriately is very important in generating a domain-specific solution shell. An example of such a rule set would be all the rules that are necessary to identify that there is a need to tune a particular distributed control system in a process plant.

Inheritance Mechanisms

Other methodologies that have been found to be important in the construction of domain-dependent solution shells for the manufacturing and process industries, as well as other industrial sectors, stem from declarative knowledge representation in the form of inheritance mechanisms (see Figure 6-5). Given that you have organized the declarative component as a collection of knowledge classes, it becomes important to define a taxonomy in which higher up in the taxonomy you have the general information that is common to all sites and lower down in the taxonomy at the instance level you have the site-specific information.

A fundamental methodology is to acquire the site-specific information through a knowledge acquisition process that generates the instances for that particular location. Inheritance mechanisms are ideally suited to build in this knowledge-base flexibility. You should view this methodology as completing, specifying, and rounding out the declarative component of the knowledge base on a site-specific basis. It is a process that will take place by using an intelligent, easy-to-use knowledge acquisition front end during a field installation process when the domain-specific shell arrives at a specific site.

Rule Writing

There are important techniques that are used to write the rules that support a domain-specific solution shell. First, it is very important to be able to write your rules in a flexible format so that pattern match-

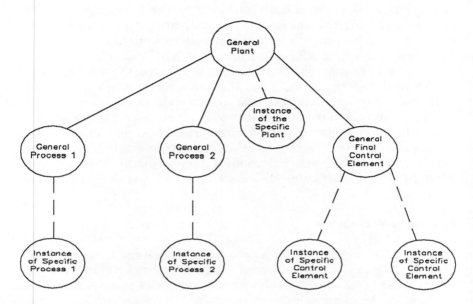

Figure 6-5   Process-oriented inheritance structure in the declarative component of the knowledge base.

ing can pick up the important site-specific bindings that have been acquired through the field installation process. Basically, with this concept you do not use specific numbers or specific symbols for any piece of logic in writing the rules. For instance, do not assume that everyone has a maximum number of 10 tanks at a particular plant. The number of tanks at a particular plant would be acquired during the field installation process and instantiated as an instance schema in some knowledge class someplace in the inheritance taxonomy. Rules should pattern match from the instance schema to acquire the specifics with respect to a particular site. Writing rules in a general and flexible format that are made specific by the acquisition of the site-specific information is a key mechanism to generating a domain-specific shell.

In addition to the concept of general rules as opposed to specific rules, another important technique in building domain-specific shells is embodied by the concept of rules that write rules. Most heuristic environments are built around incremental compilation techniques. This allows you to reconfigure on the fly and to exploit optimizations not only at compile time but at run time as well. Quite often, the best way to capture the logic necessary in a domain-specific shell is to write a meta rule that is a template for the actual run-time rule that would be optimal for a particular site.

After the field installation process is completed, the expert system begins a procedure of allowing the meta rules to pattern match against the instantiated site-specific knowledge base. The result of this pattern matching, when a meta rule is allowed to fire, is the compilation of an optimal site-specific rule. Rules that write rules can add great power, flexibility, and run-time performance to a domain-specific shell. You can view the concept of rules that write rules as analogous to the concept of a LISP macro versus a LISP defun. Code generation is an important concept to be aware of as a technique and methodology for developing a highly efficient domain-specific shell.

The Use of Forms

There are a number of tools that are important in building domain-specific shells. I have built domain-specific shells for the process and manufacturing industries, publishing, MIS, and government systems. In all cases, the same general facilities were needed. A key aspect in building a domain-specific shell is the ability to acquire the site-specific knowledge in an easy manner. The goal of the domain-specific shell is to solve a particular problem such as intelligent alarm management or tuning distributed controllers for processes without requiring deep computer science or artificial intelligence knowledge from the user. To do this, you must have a flexible form system, a graphically oriented knowledge-base editor, and a restricted-domain natural-language processor. When the shell shows up at a particular site, an individual who is familiar with the domain and responsible for putting that shell to work will sit down with the knowledge-acquisition interface.

By a simple process of drawing, filling out forms, and answering questions through the natural-language processor, the shell is field installed and made specific to that particular location. Forms are particularly useful to capture site-specific information. You can view a form as a presentation mechanism of a graphical representation that is textually oriented for a particular knowledge-base schema. Essentially, by filling out the form, you are filling out and completing a schema in the declarative component of the knowledge base.

Quite often it is important to acquire the site-specific configuration to a particular problem. For instance, if you are going to have an expert system that tunes control structures, you need to include in the knowledge-base the process and control topology and technology that comprises the particular plant environment. By including a graphically oriented knowledge-base editor comprised of standard "icons," you can give the user during the field installation process the ability to rapidly and graphically connect objects that represent the particular site-specific problem. Each one of these objects should be related to a knowledge class in the declarative component of the knowledge base. In particular, they would be related to one or more schemas in that knowledge class. All of the objects that are positioned on the screen should be mouse sensitive. The clicking on any object would produce a form on which the specific parameters associated with that object for that particular site would be acquired.

This mechanism of allowing the user to draw and then fill out the associated forms with the particular objects that have been positioned is highly productive, and it efficiently acquires the site-specific information. There will be opportunities and necessities for the expert system to ask questions of the user during the field installation process and to accept appropriate replies. A tool that best captures this in the spirit of a domain-specific shell is a restricted-domain language processor. Through the combination of sophisticated form systems, graphically oriented knowledge-base editors, and natural-language processing, you can present a very nice and easy-to-use knowledge acquisition interface for the shell.

Stable Storage Architecture

A final tool and methodology that is absolutely necessary in the architecture, design, and implementation of a domain-specific shell is the concept and provision for a stable storage architecture (see Figure 6-6). It is important to organize all of the site-specific knowledge, as well as the overall system, in an MIS database-like fashion. While reasoning, the application should be able to retrieve on demand from the database any knowledge and information necessary. An absolutely ideal candidate for such a stable storage architecture is Digital's relational database Rdb. By incorporating a database such as Rdb into the implementation of the domain-specific shell, you can provide for a much improved overall solution with greater flexibility and extensibility.

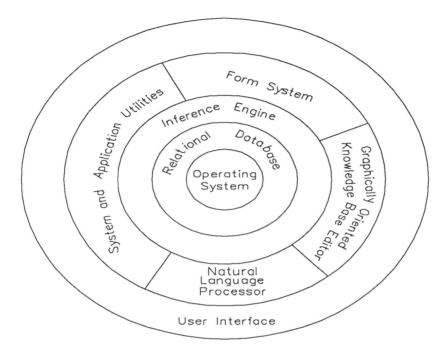

Figure 6-6   Software architecture of a domain-specific solution shell.

In the domain-specific solution shells that I have built over the years I have tended to make the stable storage architecture as central to the overall application as possible. This means that reporting, as well as history functionality, ad hoc queries, and the like are actually being conducted against the database kernel of the shell. Only intelligent reasoning is reserved for the in-memory knowledge base provided by an inference engine.

Conclusion

The VAX, with its many layered software products and the VAX calling standard provides an ideal environment for the construction of domain-specific solution shells. In general, it is a good idea to use as many off the shelf tools and facilities as possible. In addition to Rdb, there are many other products that will greatly reduce the time to development and the associated cost of the overall shell. There exist many form and graphical systems as well as other utilities and facilities. By combining these facilities intelligently, you can obtain a high-quality environment that is uniquely qualified to solve a particular class group of problems in a very flexible fashion.

7

Knowledge Engineering and Project Organization

The Myths and Realities

Historically, there has been a common mental image associated with the building of expert systems. This image is one of incremental development performed by an individual who is commonly referred to as a knowledge engineer. Supposedly, you find a bright AI computer science person and provide him or her with an expert system shell tool such as one of the readily found industrial products available today like OPS5 or ART. This individual then interacts with a domain expert to acquire the knowledge necessary to construct the expert system.

Over a period of time the knowledge base incrementally takes shape with criticism and refinement directing the incremental development as provided by the domain expert. Over the years in the projects that I have developed in the process industries, CIM industries, graphic arts, and the like I have found this procedure wholly inadequate. There is a broad spectrum of types of expert systems. These range from simple small knowledge systems containing a few rules and objects to very large and complicated integrated, time-critical expert systems containing extensive functionality and logic for a particular problem domain (see Figure 7-1). The commonly held-to procedure of

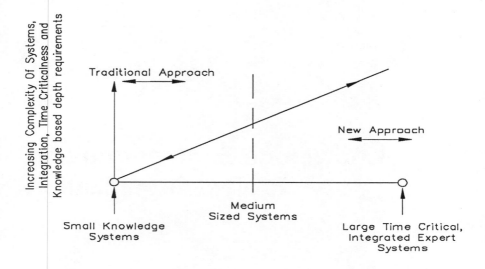

Figure 7-1   Continuous spectrum of knowledge-based applications.

incremental development seems to be ideally suited for small knowledge systems and falls totally apart and becomes an unusable methodology for large real-time expert systems.

The notion associated with incremental development is that you can continually refine and add knowledge to the knowledge base until the expert system is reproducing the logic of a particular domain expert faithfully enough to be deployed. In reality, the architecture and design of expert systems becomes as highly stylized as that used in the development of traditional applications. It takes as much time to program control structures such as rule sets, declarative agendas, and knowledge class mechanisms in an expert system as it does to program in a traditional application. The ad hoc procedure of architecture, design, and implementation associated with incremental development leads to an unwieldy, unstructured application that is extremely difficult to maintain, modify, integrate, and extend as new requirements become necessary.

It is unrealistic to assume that one individual has the time, energy, and wherewithal to not only do the programming, computer science, architecture, and design that is necessary but to interact strongly and efficiently with one or more domain experts associated with the problem that is being automated. This notion is just absolutely out of line with most large-scale meaningful problems that need to be addressed in industry today.

There are technical issues that motivate and foster the need for new paradigms of architecture, design, and development as well as knowledge engineering and project organization. Most of the applications that are of great interest to vertical markets have severe integration requirements. These applications require the utilization of many technologies as well as many tools to provide a satisfactory solution. In addition, many of the problems are too large and complicated to be conveniently modeled and automated as a single expert system. The process industries are characteristic of the requirement for a cooperating expert system approach. In the process operations, there are a number of issues that need to be dealt with in an intelligent fashion. Unless you break up the automation problem and the intelligence problem into multiple manageable pieces such as an intelligent statistical process control system, an intelligent alarm management system, and an intelligent supervisory control and parametric optimization system, you cannot have any hope of great success. Distribution becomes a key aspect in most delivery environments because of the intense CPU nature of expert systems as well as the data requirements and high availability and fault tolerance requirements.

Further technology issues provide motivation for finding a new approach to knowledge engineering and project organization. These include the requirements of building a domain-dependent solution shell and solving the problems associated with time criticalness of the overall AI application.

These technology issues that are real-world requirements given the nature of the current medium- to large-scale expert system opportunities motivate an entirely different organizational structure and methodology for architecting, designing, and delivering expert-system-based solutions to problems.

Characterization of the Two Different Approaches

Many organizations have tried attacking certain problems with the pure knowledge engineering approach. The result, by and large, has been demonstration or prototype solutions as opposed to delivered and deployed systems. Quite often project teams have found that once an environment has been accepted as meaningful, in order to meet the real industrial issues a complete and total rewrite of the system would be necessary. Time and time again this has manifested itself with expert systems not being deployed because of the shock to management of finding that what they have after a significant investment is really nothing more than an interesting proof of feasibility.

It has become fairly obvious to many organizations and project teams that a different approach is necessary to address medium- to large-scale expert systems, that as much attention to detail, design, systems logic, and control logic is required in these heuristic applications as in the large and complicated traditional ones that have proceeded them.

The Usual Approach

The usual approach of knowledge engineering and project organization is best suited for problems that have a loose integration requirement and a more offline flavor to their run-time characteristics. This basic approach is one of bottom-up development. New rules and schemas are added incrementally, as knowledge is extracted from a particular domain expert, without a real structured plan as to how the overall problem will be solved. The method is usually referred to as the "knowledge engineering approach." Associated with it is a whole culture of mental images and methodologies for doing things. In systems like this, you are usually aiming for accuracies that are in the neighborhood of 90 percent or less. It is not expected that the expert system will be absolutely flawless in everything that it does. This stems from its basic operational utilization mode that is loose and not of an autonomous flavor. Ideally, this approach should be used for small knowledge systems that could be described in under 100 rules and 100 objects. Usually associated with this approach is a lack of a formal architecture, design, and implementation process. It is one of piecing together a system by iterative refinement.

The New Approach

This approach might be best characterized as top down because the first step is to scientifically analyze how things are done and the best way to do them. It is a hybrid method, a combination of traditional programming and some AI methods that are carryovers from the purely knowledge engineering approach. The new approach should be used for a class group of problems that have tight integration requirements and a strong flavor of online, real-time criticalness. It is for problems in which the expert system is going to be embedded in an overall applications environment and in which that expert system must be capable of responding meaningfully on a transaction-by-transaction basis. This approach is usually used when you are striving for an expert system that is 100 percent accurate in what it does, which is necessary given its time-critical, integrated, and online flavor. It would be used for large time-critical expert systems that have to be embedded in an online sense into an overall applications and systems environment (see Figure 7-2).

A final motivation for a new knowledge engineering project organization paradigm stems from the common myth that a data-driven inference engine allows you to add knowledge willy nilly as new things are discovered. This common assumption is quite often related to the notion of opportunistic programming, in which you can add rules to describe new functionality on an incremental basis. Unfortunately, except in small knowledge systems, this myth is totally untrue and dangerous. In the solution to a problem such as scheduling or maintenance there indeed exists an algorithm that leads to a solution. Even if you are approaching the solution heuristically and it con-

	Common	New
Problems	Loose integration Not time critical	Tight Integration Time critical
Approach	Bottom up	Top down
Method	Traditional Knowledge Engineering	Traditional Software Engineering plus AI methods
Accuracy	90 %	100 %
Used For	Small Knowledge Systems	Large Real Time Integrated Expert Systems

Figure 7-2 The common knowledge engineering approach vs. the new systematic approach.

tains some aspects of nondeterministic logic in the solution, you are still confronted with structuring the knowledge base to efficiently arrive at answers. I can think of only a few examples of expert system applications for which adding rules incrementally and in parallel with no attention to detail or to how the knowledge base schedules its reasoning can lead to a successful expert system application.

Using the New Approach

In building an integrated artificial-intelligence-based scheduling system, you have to pay great attention to how things execute during a trace through the application. Logic has to be encoded in the knowledge base to allow it to intelligently focus its attention. It is necessary to break up that knowledge base into meaningful and manageable subsegments using techniques such as rule sets and declarative agendas to control the order of execution of logic. When you look at a heuristic application and then audit the amount of time spent in developing it, you will see that the myth associated with incremental development becomes exposed rather easily. The fact that an expert system requires structuring of algorithmic information does not diminish its heuristic component or its AI content. An expert system is not less heuristic if it requires clean packaging and scheduling of logic in order for it to arrive at an efficient solution. This merely implies that there is a large collection of AI applications that are not best solved by a purely opportunistic programming philosophy.

Conduct an Audit

It is important for an organization to first conduct an audit of all the opportunities to understand clearly the characteristics associated with those opportunities. This is necessary to decide whether the new methodology or the old one might be best applied (see Figure 7-3). You must understand how you are going to access the knowledge necessary to construct the expert system and know whether this knowledge can be successfully garnered from a single expert or if it will require a number of experts spread across a number of sites. It is also critical to understand the underlying time constraints associated with the solution of the problem. If these time constraints are loose and long in duration, you have a better chance to solve it with the traditional

Domain and Problem Selection Issues

- Audit of opportunities
- Access to knowledge
- Time constraints & constants
- Common sense reasoning
- Expectation management
- Learning requirements
- Justification & explanation requirements
- Integration & system requirements
- User interface requirements
- Database requirements
- Knowledge base requirements
- Development requirements
- Delivery requirements

Figure 7-3 Key issues in knowledge-based systems.

knowledge engineering approach. However, if the time constants are short and the decision making and reasoning is complicated, a willy-nilly approach more often than not will lead to an unsatisfactory result.

You must understand what depth of common-sense reasoning, if any, is going to be necessary. It is very important to understand this beforehand and to have a methodology and design for either eliminating it altogether or for dealing with it in an intelligent fashion. In properly selecting a problem to address, it is critical to choose one in which expectation management is a natural and easy thing to accomplish. The mere words "artificial intelligence" or "expert systems" conjure up mental images of silicone brains. It is bad enough that the problems are difficult to automate reliably given the current state of the art; it is even worse if the expectations of management or a customer are way out of line with what can be delivered. Unless proper expectation management can be conducted, the project is liable to run into great difficulties.

Learning requirements for any particular problem or domain must be understood up front with a mechanism and paradigm for addressing it. There are a number of different ways to get an expert system to learn, which increases the complexity of the underlying architecture and design. If the system is going to have any justification and explanation facilities, they must be assessed clearly in light of the present state of technology. One of the great claims associated with expert systems is that they can conveniently explain why they make a certain decision. The claim is quite often better than the reality in an implemented system. Implementing a justification and explanation facility is a very challenging set of activities. Requirements in this area can lead to serious complications if unrealistic expectations are set.

Integration and Systems Requirements

One of the most significant issues to access up front is any and all integration and system requirements. This area is greatly overlooked by most people in developing knowledge-based solutions to problems. It is often almost thought of as low-level plumbing that someone will do later on in some fashion. In reality many of the toughest problems associated with building a deployable high-quality heuristic application are associated with these systems issues. Likewise people tend to minimize the complexities associated with user-interface requirements. Much effort can be expended if these requirements are not clearly understood and addressed.

Very few expert systems that will solve medium to large problems in an online sense are capable of doing so without having severe traditional database requirements. These requirements might range from accessing existing data to overcoming the limitations of current expert system shell technology. Database requirements need to be understood up front as clearly as possible in the selection of a domain as well as of a particular problem in that domain. You must try to understand the knowledge-base requirements not only from the viewpoint of heuristic reasoning but as they relate to explanation and reporting requirements more in line with traditional database technology. Often you are confronted with the requirement that the knowledge base must perform the services of intelligent inference-based reasoning and also those associated with a high-quality traditional database system. Unless you properly understand the requirements that are going to be placed on the knowledge base, you can choose a problem and solve it with a methodology that will lead to disastrous consequences.

Development and Delivery Requirements

Finally, it becomes critical to understand clearly the development requirements as well as the delivery requirements. The closer these two match each other, the more efficient the overall solution and the project effort itself will be.

The key aspect to the new knowledge engineering and project organization approach is having a clear methodology to choose domains as well as problems in domains to solve. Unless you ask all of the above questions, you cannot have a clear understanding of the depth of the problem or the solution requirements to solve it. If you choose the wrong problem up front and then compound it by choosing the wrong approach such as the traditional knowledge engineering approach, you are almost guaranteed to have a failure. The algorithm for doing domain and problem selection will allow you to rank and categorize your problems ranging from small knowledge systems to large real-time, highly integrated expert systems. You can then intelligently decide which problems to attack and which knowledge engineering and project organization methodology to use.

The New Organizational Structure

In the new organization structure seven types of individuals are needed to successfully build large-scale knowledge-based applications (see Figure 7-4). This is in contrast with the usual method that basically requires two, domain experts and knowledge engineers.

The first is a project manager who is capable of organizing the others to work in parallel. The manager must be familiar with most of the technology and the issues, and the domain in general. Unless the right type of manager is chosen, the team will wander aimlessly, never producing a successful project or product.

The next type is a new type of knowledge engineer. This is an individual who is familiar with the domain as well as the paradigms of knowledge-based reasoning and who can interact strongly with the real domain experts. But this engineer does not actually implement the knowledge base. It is better to find domain experts and teach

- The Project Managers
- The New Knowledge Engineers
- The AI Systems Engineers
- The AI Software Engineers
- The Traditional Application Engineers
- The Traditional Computer Scientists
- The Domain Experts
- The Orthogonal Domain Sites

Figure 7-4 Key components of an organization structure.

them the paradigms of AI than it is to take computer scientists and make them domain experts.

Large knowledge-based applications that have a strong integration and time-critical requirement need a lot of services that are removed from the actual intelligent reasoning component of the application. These services span the areas of integration, cooperation, distribution, parametrization, and time criticalness.

The third type is an artificial intelligence systems engineer. This person will concentrate on providing system services to the knowledge-based application and is someone who understands AI and knowledge bases well and systems engineering and operating systems in general.

The fourth type is an artificial intelligence software engineer. This person understands AI, expert systems, and knowledge-based techniques intimately and is very familiar with programming requirements for intelligent reasoning applications.

In the new method, the AI software engineers interact strongly with the new knowledge engineers to understand the domain. The new knowledge engineers garner their knowledge from the actual domain experts. The AI systems engineers provide services to the AI software engineers and interact with them strongly.

The fifth type is a traditional application engineer to deal with integration and systems requirements needed in a particular vertical market. This engineer understands the intimate details of dealing with hardware and software that is characteristic of that particular domain. For instance, in the process control industries the engineer would understand how distributed control systems work and what it takes to be able to integrate with them in a meaningful fashion.

The sixth is a traditional computer scientist. Much procedural and traditional code, as well as other computer-related issues, are required to build these types of systems. This work is best served by people who specialize in traditional computer science.

The seventh type is the actual domain expert who is a specialist in the problem that is being attacked. Domain experts are key to a successful project. The new knowledge engineers who are the full-time in-house domain experts associated with the project interact with the outside domain experts in an efficient manner. Large-scale problems usually require more than one domain expert to be successful. Coordinating, managing, and distilling down the information from these multiple sources becomes a key task of the new knowledge engineers.

Finally, the last entities in the new organization structure are the orthogonal domain sites. In building a knowledge-based solution to a large, real-time integrated problem, it becomes necessary to decide up front whether the solution is going to be a one-shot expert system or a domain-specific solution shell. If the requirement is for a domain-specific solution shell, a small set of orthogonal sites that can provide the contrast of knowledge necessary to address the problem in a more generic sense must be identified and chosen very carefully.

In large to medium problems the completed team might span a number of individuals. I have been associated with projects that involved as many as 20 individuals working simultaneously and in parallel to produce a high-quality solution in this format. It is through this organizational structure that you can build large teams of individuals to address tough heuristic problems in reasonable time frames.

The New Systematic Approach

The Audit

After you have built the recommended project organizational structure, there is an associated new approach that is necessary for successful large-scale expert system projects and products (see Figure 7-5). The first task is to perform a detailed domain and problem audit. This is necessary not only to select the appropriate problem to address but to guarantee a knowledge engineering and project organization

- Problem & Domain Audit
- Feasibility Study — Tiger Team
    - The level 1 prototype

      Where is the AI
    - The Team, resources and the Macro Plan
- Review & Expectation management
- The Level II prototype
    - Large AI content
    - Systems requirements
    - Prototype all issues that can be identified
- Review & Expectation management
- Project Management
    - The expanded team
    - The resources
    - Micro plan
- Review & Expectation management

Figure 7-5   The systematic approach and checklist for the new methodology.

approach that will guarantee a high probability of success. This audit should address the areas mentioned above and should result in a detailed study that characterizes and rates the various problems in terms of their difficulties and attributes in a comparative sense. The study that results from the problem and domain audit should map onto the necessary knowledge engineering and project organizational requirements that will allow success to take place.

Feasibility Study

In the next phase you should build a team of individuals to conduct a detailed feasibility study. In this feasibility study you should construct a level I prototype to clearly delineate where the AI content is and what its nature is likely to be. The study should clearly address the necessary team resources and schedule that will be required to successfully address the problem. Essentially you are putting together a macro plan and beginning to learn a little about the requirements of addressing the opportunity. Then you should make a detailed review of the feasibility study and of management expectations. All too often expert system projects have met with unfavorable results because of unwieldy management or customer expectations. It is important to ascertain early what can be done and to make sure all parties have clear expectations.

The Level II Prototype

The next phase is enlarging the prototype to have a larger AI content. You are still in a learning process, still groping to discover how to solve and best structure the problem. You are keenly looking for algorithms, procedural or heuristic, that might be intelligently applied in the knowledge base. It is in this phase that you need to begin addressing systems requirements, doing so in a way that incorporates them in the prototype to allow an assessment of the detail and complications that might follow. It is a good idea to prototype all issues that can be identified with the problem that you are attempting to automate. All too often people assume in knowledge-based projects that something will be easy or is well understood, only to find out later that is well understood in traditional programming environments and not well understood in heuristic programming environments.

Upon the successful conclusion of the level II prototype there should be another review meeting that again presents in a codified form all of the findings. Again expectation management is key. The level II prototype will elucidate new issues. The document that is delivered with this prototype should present reasonable approaches to solving them.

Detailed Project Management

Upon the successful review meeting, you must begin building the real team in a meaningful fashion. In this phase of the systematic approach the team needs to be expanded into the real team as indicated in the organizational structure that was presented above. In addition there must be enough people in each class to deliver the knowledge-based application in the specified time frame. In this phase the resources that will be necessary to deliver the project or product must be clearly identified. Finally a detailed micro plan should be constructed that should be an outgrowth of the macro plan and the results that were found in constructing the level II prototype.

The micro plan should be presented by the project management team at a review meeting. This plan should be scrutinized in great detail to make sure that all assumptions are true and that no issues that could jeopardize the project or product have been left unaddressed.

The Real Development Begins

At this point you might feel that to a certain degree this is the traditional knowledge engineering approach. It is. It is used to understand enough about the problem so that you know exactly how you are going to solve it, not because you have hopes of delivering the prototype systems as real industrial-strength capability. In this phase you should put aside all prototype work, considering that it has been done from the viewpoint of understanding how you are going to solve the problem and what issues need to be addressed (see Figure 7-6).

In this phase you should now know enough to sit down and develop a detailed architecture, design, and implementation document that could pass scrutiny by traditional software engineering approaches. In addition you should be designing any needed tools and simulations that you have identified by the previous work. Here you depart radically from traditional knowledge engineering approaches. You are not going to merely incrementally refine the prototypes and let them loose on the world; you are going to put them aside and with careful precision and science design and address systematically a solution to the heuristic problem. It is usually very hard to get off the shell all of the facilities that you will need for a particular project. Therefore, it becomes important to design up front and early the missing pieces of systems technology that will be necessary to solve the problem.

The detailed architecture, design, and implementation document should be presented at a review meeting. At this point a no-go or go decision can be made scientifically. If the decision is to proceed with

- The real thing
    - start over with detailed analysis and design
    - Design needed tools & simulations
- Review & Expectation management
- Real Implementation stage
- Review & Expectation management
- Testing
- Review & Expectation management
- Improvements, bug fixes, worm fixes and knowledge tuning
- Review & Expectation management
- Deployment of production systems
- Review of Project
- Transfer of responsibilities
    - maintenance
    - improvements

Figure 7-6   The systematic approach and checklist for the new methodology (continued).

the project as outlined, the next phase of the systematic approach to developing large-scale expert systems ensues.

The Real Implementation Stage

Implementation of the real capability now begins. This implementation is conducted by members of the new organizational structure. By using concepts associated with cooperating expert systems and integrated AI, you can have many people working on the project in parallel at the same time. Moreover, if you choose not to build cooperating expert systems, you can still modularize a single application using techniques such as rule sets and knowledge classes. In any event, in this phase you begin implementing what has been specified in the detailed analysis and design document. If it turns out that any code fragments in the level I or II prototypes can be used, do so. However, you should not try to force reusability of prototype code in the real system.

During the implementation cycle, you should have a number of review meetings to carefully and iteratively refine the structured design and architecture plans and to approve changes to them. Control over the project becomes absolutely necessary, not only source code control but architecture and design control. You must treat these projects as though you are building a house with formal blueprints and civil engineering diagrams. This becomes critical when a number of people are attacking a heuristic project. Every rule must be controlled, as well as every schema. There must be no ad hoc changes to the fundamental design of the system, interface, or control logic.

When the first version of the system is successfully implemented, detailed testing must start. In the traditional knowledge engineering approach, you present the expert system to the domain expert for criticism and subsequent refinement. In this new systematic approach, it is necessary to build a test suite to automate the testing of the logic that is implemented in the overall application, as well as to test the knowledge base itself. This test suite should be designed by the new knowledge engineers in conjunction with the actual domain experts and the AI software and systems engineers. The results of testing should be presented at a detailed review meeting. This review meeting should authorize any changes in the fundamental design or implementation.

The next phase in the systematic approach involves making approved improvements to the application and fixing bugs. It is in this phase that tightly controlled knowledge tuning takes place. Even though you are attempting to build an expert system application using traditional software engineering techniques, you are still confronted with the fact that problems in this class group are not as regular and well defined as traditional ones. This will impose a higher degree of flexibility on being able to rapidly tune knowledge and representation in a controlled sense than what might be expected with well-described traditional applications. Once the improvements, bug fixes, and knowledge tuning have been successful, a review meeting should be conducted to formalize the process of deployment.

At this point, the expert system application is ready for deployment in a production environment. If the expert system was properly architected and designed to support the proper modes of use, deployment of the expert system is a natural and straightforward operation. The design of the expert system should allow deployment in parallel with existing operational methodologies. In the first phase of deployment, you are essentially doing advanced testing. If this is successful, the deployed application can be used in lieu of existing approaches. Deployment can be more or less critical depending upon the mode of operation of the expert system. For instance, deployment is more complicated for an autonomous expert system that is tightly coupled into the feedback loop of a process than it is for a highly interactive adviser that does not make automatic decisions. However, those facilities necessary to make the deployment a natural process would have been designed into the project.

Upon the successful deployment of the knowledge-based application, you should conduct a detailed review of the overall project. This is necessary to understand scientifically how to do it better the next time. Finally, a transfer of responsibilities should ensue to allow ongoing maintenance and improvements to the application using scientific and controlled software engineering methods. More often than not, the developers of the application will not be the long-term maintainers and improvers. Properly structuring a transfer of responsibilities with a strict code management and feature management structure is essential to the long-term success of the application. As is the case with all software, modifications, bug fixes, and feature enhancements become necessary over time. Only by having a systematic approach, as formal as the ones associated with traditional applications, can you hope to keep the knowledge base current, manageable, and maintainable by individuals who are not geared to research and development.

Tool Selection

A fundamental issue and problem that most organizations face is that of selecting the shells or tools necessary to build an expert system application (see Figure 7-7). In the small knowledge system class of problem, it usually results in the selection of an expert system shell tool. This can be a challenging problem in and of itself. This problem is compounded dramatically when you are addressing medium to large time-critical expert system applications. The following procedure results in a high degree of reliability in making correct tool selections. It requires a good knowledge of how you are going to solve the

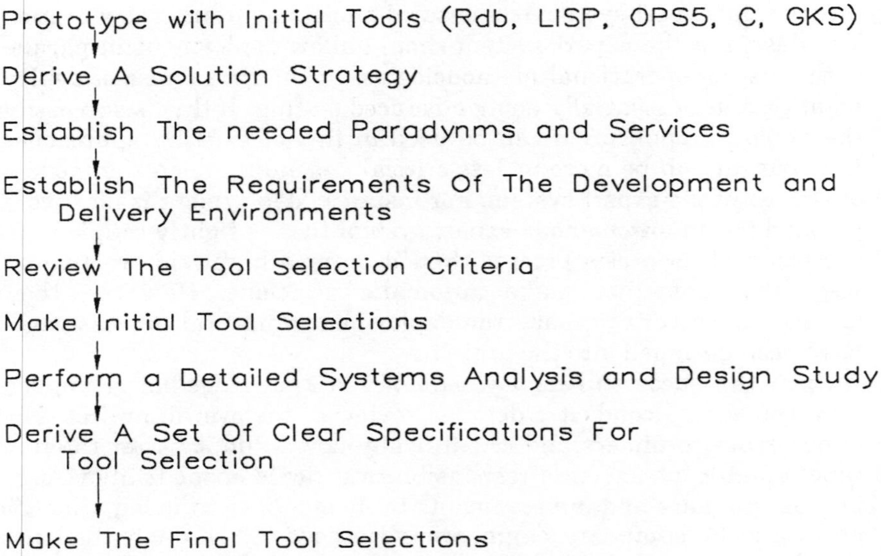

Prototype with Initial Tools (Rdb, LISP, OPS5, C, GKS)

↓

Derive A Solution Strategy

↓

Establish The needed Paradynms and Services

↓

Establish The Requirements Of The Development and
    Delivery Environments

↓

Review The Tool Selection Criteria

↓

Make Initial Tool Selections

↓

Perform a Detailed Systems Analysis and Design Study

↓

Derive A Set Of Clear Specifications For
    Tool Selection

↓

Make The Final Tool Selections

Figure 7-7 The process of selecting tools.

problem and a detailed understanding of all of the issues that need to be addressed.

First, prototype using your best guess at tools. For instance, on the VAX, you might choose Rdb, Digital's relational database; VAX LISP, Digital's implementation of common LISP; OPS5, Digital's data-driven inference engine; C; and GKS, Digital's device-independent graphics device driver. The process of prototyping using these first guesses about tools will eventually lead to a solution strategy. This solution strategy will allow the project team to codify the necessary paradigms and services that will be required to solve the problem in an intelligent fashion.

This is followed by a detailed analysis in understanding development and delivery environments and requirements. When these issues are understood, the organization can review the tools that were chosen for the initial prototype and contrast them with other tools that might better meet the requirements of the project.

This leads to an initial tool selection. This tool selection shows what might be accomplished. Part of this tool selection might include tools that are not readily available off the shelf but that the organization feels it can develop as part of the solution to the problem. This initial tool selection is followed by making a detailed systems analysis and design document that structures the whole application effort in a traditional software engineering context. The results of this analysis are a formal set of specifications, features, and functionality for the resultant large-scale expert system. This specification leads to a final tool selection process.

Addressing large problems requires the combining of a number of tools to arrive at a satisfactory solution using minimum development dollars. The tool selection is not trivial. Selecting a tool a priori and sticking with it through deployment is sometimes an accomplishable goal when you are developing a small knowledge system. It is a dangerous policy when you are attempting to build medium- to large-scale expert systems.

The VAX with its associated layered hardware and software, as well as its project management and software management facilities, provides an absolutely ideal environment in which to address large-scale time-critical integrated expert system problems. The tools on the VAX allow you to take an integrated approach naturally and easily. Its excellent communication facilities allow distribution requirements to be dealt with meaningfully. Its wide selection of traditional tools that can be integrated with heuristic tools allows domain-specific shells to be naturally constructed. Right from the beginning, if you are going to use the new systematic approach to knowledge engineering and project organization, you should automate that process on the VAX using as many project management, software maintenance, and operational and developmental aids as possible. If you view the development of expert systems as a mystery and an art to be conducted in a willy-nilly fashion, you are going to miss the fundamental opportunity that the VAX environment presents for these types of problems; that opportunity is to be able to automate meaningfully the new organizational structure, as well as the systematic approach, in a step-and-repeat reproducible fashion.

8

Tools

Overview

Artificial intelligence has become a real industrial technology. It has moved out of the university environment into mainstream industry at large. This has happened because of two industrial factors. First, there is a broad spectrum of readily available software tools that allows development teams to reliably construct meaningful prototypes and product that have an AI content. Secondly, the hardware platforms have become sufficiently powerful at a greatly reduced cost. Not too long ago artificial intelligence was relegated completely to the university environment and, at best, was experimental software that was highly suspect as to its reliability and regularity. In addition, doing any meaningful research or development required the use of a very large computer at a great cost.

Because of those two factors, AI remained in the university for many years. With the industrial development of microelectronics, very powerful computational environments could be produced by traditional vendors at a fraction of the cost of the older technology. Moreover, heuristic and symbolic programming environments underwent radical development and enhancement since their dawn in the mid-1950s. LISP itself, which has its roots in the fifties, underwent significant experimental research and developmental evolution throughout the sixties, seventies, and early eighties. A significant event was the pulling

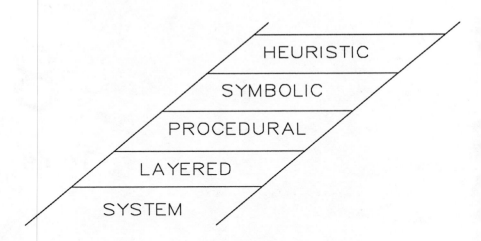

Figure 8-1 The tool ladder.

together of the many flavors and types of LISPs into a common LISP standard. Common LISP represents a maturing of the technology and a meaningful attempt toward industrial standardization and portability. It is a clear sign on the part of academics, industry at large, and the government that they are going to make artificial intelligence a technology that can be relied on for real project and product development.

There are many tools that exist to produce either prototypes, deliverable projects, or generic products. These tools might be characterized as either procedural, symbolic, heuristic, layered, or system (see Figure 8-1). An important concept to focus on, when talking about tools as they relate to the VAX, is the solution flavor as opposed to the specific-purpose flavor of a VAX. The VAX is a solutions machine. In order to accomplish sophisticated high performance and natural results, it is important to blend together various tools and facilities to accomplish a given task at hand. All too often, developers tend to use a VAX as a LISP machine or an OPS5 machine and try to stay within the cozy confines of a particular paradigm of computation. This is directly in contrast with the philosophy of DEC computation and more often than not leads to frustrated developers and unsuccessful projects or products.

In particular, if you are attempting to build an application in the form of a domain-specific solution shell, the motivations are even stronger for a multiple tool approach to accomplish the task at hand.

In the selection of tools, it becomes critical to understand the goals of the development effort. If the goals are merely to generate throwaway code of a prototype nature, proper tool selection becomes less important. If, however, you are attempting to deliver a solution, the tool selection should be an outgrowth of a detailed architectural, design, and implementation study. Applications that are targeted for the process industries, general manufacturing, finance, and various government arenas will require a multiple tool approach on the VAX.

Procedural Tools

All too often development teams who are attempting to build knowledge-based solutions to problems feel that traditional procedural tools such as Fortran or C detract from the AI orientation and spirit of the endeavor. This is in direct opposition to the spirit of the solution philosophy on a VAX. An illustration is the requirement for computing a fast Fourier transform to do power spectrum analysis of a particular time domain signal. This computation is exceedingly compute intensive. Moreover, it is a well understood computationally and by and large already exists in high-performance traditional languages such as Fortran, C, and even assembler.

The spirit on the VAX would be to use one of these traditional procedural languages in a way that would allow the calculation to be manipulated, used, controlled, and reasoned about from other various symbolic and heuristic environments. For instance, it should be natural to call on an FFT from either the right-hand or the left-hand side of a rule that is sitting in an inference engine-based heuristic computing environment.

When you consider using procedural tools in the development of a knowledge-based solution, you must look at a number of advantages. First, applications already exist that perform meaningful functionality that would be exceedingly costly to reimplement under a different computational paradigm. Second, given the nature of the computation, a traditional language might provide a higher-quality solution than one that could be obtained with a symbolic or heuristic computation. In addition to the above, more often than not, when you attack a medium-to-large-sized application, you will find that a multiprocess, if not a multicomputer, approach best serves the performance and architectural requirements. This being the case, the need to be able to build a single executable image is removed. It is highly likely on the VAX that you are going to use extensive interprocess communications to pull together all of the various modules into a single cognitive solution. These interprocess communications might be accomplished by such methods as simple mail boxes or by using a more sophisticated transaction-based model. In cooperating expert systems, you might choose a blackboard architecture for the knowledge interchange protocol between the various modules.

The point is that you are usually going to end up with a multiprocess approach. This reduces the pressures to code all of the application in a single symbolic or heuristic environment that is capable of producing a single executable image. By using large and extensive amounts of traditional procedural code when appropriate, you can greatly accelerate the development cycle of a particular project, as well as the effective use of the underlying hardware platform. Moreover, in certain areas such as government systems, there are mandates as to what languages can be used. Presently, for defense work, ADA is a standard. The only other recognized standard is common LISP, a symbolic language. Whatever the motivation, you should not shy away from traditional procedural languages but rather view them as meaningful opportunities to produce a result more quickly and easily, with better overall characteristics than what could be obtained with the common approach of using a single knowledge engineering environment in which to solve the whole problem.

Symbolic Tools

There are a number of key aspects that differentiate symbolic computing environments from traditional procedural environments. Primarily, they involve data abstraction and procedure abstraction. The two most commonly referred to symbolic environments are PROLOG and LISP. Both of these have their various advantages and disadvantages over traditional software architectures.

There are many uses for both of these languages. They span application logic, as well as systems logic. More often than not, most people use LISP or view LISP as a symbolic language with the flexibility and paradigms of computation to build sophisticated intelligent systems; this is true. However, every problem and application is best served by building an operating system for that application that would sit on top of something like VMS on the VAX. Using an environment like LISP to build the operating system to the application is a very natural path to take. LISP is an ideal system programming language because of its procedure and data abstraction. The key to using symbolic environments is to reserve them for their truly symbolic nature and to allow them to make extensive calls on other facilities and services that are computed using more traditional procedural environments.

It is important to note that you can use a language like LISP in many different ways. If you so chose, you could code LISP routines to very closely mimic a Fortran style as opposed to what is considered a true LISP style. This is not an abuse of the language. It is an intelligent application of the language given the goals of a specific project. On traditional architectures you can greatly improve the quality of symbolic-based computation by paying strict attention to detail with respect to both performance and garbage. It is very important to make extensive use of declarations and appropriate choices for data and procedure constructs. All too often, people commonly believe that LISP-based code on a traditional computer cannot provide high performance. This is not true. If you treat a VAX as if it were a LISP machine and do not look to optimize the code for the particular environment, you probably will have a performance problem. If, however, you optimized appropriately through the use of declarations, selection of computational primitives, and optimization of the algorithmic constructs used, you can produce a high-performance LISP-based result for those code fragments that should be kept in a language like LISP.

People often refer to the problem of garbage in the same voice as they would refer to any other insoluble problem. This also is a myth with respect to traditional hardware architectures. You can maintain your own data structures by using free list approaches and resettable cons areas to essentially obtain a garbage-free environment that is LISP based on a traditional hardware platform. It does require attention to detail and some thought before hand. However, if you are attempting to build a knowledge-based solution, you will find that the advantages of using a symbolic language like LISP on the VAX greatly outweigh the disadvantages. It is recommended that you use a LISP that adheres to the common LISP standard. This best serves the developers through the life cycle of the project. PROLOG, although an interesting language, has not met with the popularity of LISP in the

United States. Presently, LISP is by far the better choice as a symbolic environment on the VAX computational platform.

Heuristic Tools

A heuristic computational environment is one that contains a framework of intelligent reasoning, as well as the paradigms associated with building intelligent knowledge-based applications. In general, these environments might be considered to be higher level and closer to the requirements of the application than that which could be associated with LISP or PROLOG. Heuristic environments provide you with mechanisms to do data-driven computation. In traditional programming, more often than not an application is architected, designed, and implemented so that it is logic driven. This means that the logic finds the data.

In heuristic environments, by and large you are presented with the data-driven construct by which the data finds the logic. It is through this mechanism that you can obtain the benefits associated with opportunistic programming, as well as an event-driven asynchronous environment. Most of the heuristic environments that exist today are built on one of three commonly understood constructs. These are the object-oriented, inference-engine, and dependency-directed backward tracking approaches. Examples of the object-oriented approach are flavors and portable common loops. The common readily available commercial knowledge-engineering environments provide examples of the last two class groups.

All of these environments provide you with the methodology of structuring a knowledge base into a declarative component that can represent the data and the meta data and into a procedural component that can represent the operations associated with making a state transition change in the model. By and large, a knowledge base is comprised of its declarative and procedural components. The model associated with solving the problem and with the solution algorithm is contained in both the declarative and the procedural components.

Heuristic environments provide a powerful set of methodologies and models to address opportunities that require a reasoning component. However, great attention to detail is necessary in order to appropriately use them. The common myth associated with their use is that of incremental development. Often, developers are so enamored with the data-driven environment and the incremental compiler technology upon which they are built that they think that their problem can be solved by ad hoc methods that add schemas and rules to sort of sneak up on the solution to a problem. This is true when you are developing a small knowledge system. When you are developing a medium-to-large-scale system, this illusion will lead more often than not to disastrous consequences for the project or product development. In developing sophisticated applications for the process, general manufacturing, and government arenas as much attention to detail in the algorithmic design and control structure is necessary in a heuristic environment as it would be in a symbolic or traditional procedural programming language.

You must be very realistic about the limitations of these environments. If you recognize them up front and design an intelligent problem-oriented structure with a template for control, conflict resolution, and integration, you can accomplish meaningful results with these environments. Most of these environments are best served when they are coupled with other tools on the VAX. In general you pay a performance penalty for using these tools. For sophisticated modeling and reasoning constructs, the commonly available knowledge engineering environments provide excellent facilities. However, they are not cheap as far as computes on a traditional architecture are concerned. By reserving these heuristic knowledge engineering environments for the very essence of the reasoning process and then blending them in tightly with other environments such as LISP and Fortran, you can accomplish an overall high-quality solution.

Layered Tools

The great strength of the VAX computing environment is the existence of many layered software packages to address the various computational and application aspects associated with solving a real-world problem. If you tackle a problem, for instance in an area such as computer-integrated manufacturing, you are going to be confronted with the need for a traditional database, sophisticated communications, forms management, a graphics interface, numerically oriented computation, and varied and sophisticated output along many dimensions. A key insight to developing sophisticated domain-dependent solution shells on the VAX is to use as many appropriate, layered packages as is possible in the development effort.

A particularly important package is the database that will provide a stable storage architecture. A relational database is the most convenient traditional data model to couple with knowledge-based methodologies. In particular, Digital's relational base (Rdb) is ideally suited for this role. Examples of sophisticated form management systems are Digital's FMS and TDMS. These provide the environment for both capturing and presenting data in an intelligent fashion in a knowledge-based application.

Unless you are developing a knowledge-based application that will stand as an island of automation, you will find severe requirements to incorporate sophisticated communications. Digital's DECnet and their various other paradigms of communication provide an industrial-strength answer to plantwide, as well as process-specific, integration. Highly numerically intensive computations should be done in traditional languages and in layered computational packages that sit upon such programming environments as Fortran or C.

Graphics and user interfaces are always key. Extensive amounts of engineering effort can be expended in producing a user friendly and sophisticated interface to a knowledge-based application. There are many environments that exist on the VAX that can dramatically alleviate this burden.

When you are building a sophisticated knowledge-based application, you should early on identify the key programming, application, and problem-oriented facilities that will be necessary to deliver a high-quality solution. The project team should then inventory all the layered packages that are readily available directly from Digital and from third parties.

There will always be the question of a make or buy decision (see Figure 8-2). This a good question. However, most groups do not ask it and forego the great opportunity of incorporating off-the-shelf technology that already exists to produce a much higher-quality overall solution. By and large, general project teams, as well as the people associated with building knowledge-based applications, have steered away from this approach and have stayed mostly in the comfortable confines of their symbolic or heuristic environments. This has proved to be a fatal mistake for many project and product teams.

In most applications as much, if not more, time is spent in developing the various unintelligent services, computing facilities, and environments as is for those that are directly associated with the AI content. All too often development groups make the decision not to develop these necessary integration and application-oriented facilities

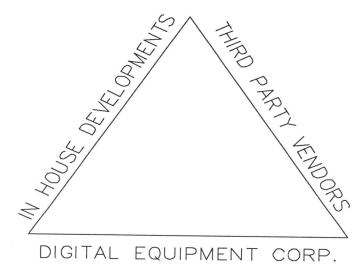

Figure 8-2 The tool triangle.

and design them away as part of the problem. This is the worst of all solutions and usually leads to an application that cannot fulfill the requirements of the real-world environment.

If you take a close look at a database environment such as Digital's Rdb and begin to understand the many facilities and services that it provides, you will soon find a spectrum of opportunities for its incorporation in almost any medium-to-large-sized knowledge-based application. The VAX computational environment, with its VMS calling standard and its general layered approach, makes the incorporation of layered products into a knowledge-based application a natural thing to do.

System Tools

Depending upon the goals of the particular project, there will be many other varied system requirements in delivering a successful solution. Some of these might be obtainable from the hardware vendor or other third parties, but a lot of them will have to be developed by the project team itself. It is recommended that every knowledge-based application has an operating system that sits between it and VMS. This application operating system will provide a central point at which to integrate intelligent services as well as to gain control over the overall application. There will be strong integration requirements. Many of these requirements can be fulfilled by existing off-the-shelf software. Some of these integration requirements will be the responsibility of the project team.

If you are going to attempt cooperating expert systems and distributed AI, you are going to be confronted with systems development work. The architecture, design, and implementation of a good domain-dependent solution shell will also require system-level facilities on the part of the project team. Time-critical artificial intelligence is always a concern when you use traditional hardware platforms. This issue can be greatly alleviated by the proper design and implementation of system facilities and services to address up front the requirement. There are a few third-party vendors who offer sophisticated packages to help in the area of systems issues. However, by and large, this will be an area of great concern to the development team. In many of the systems that have been built, it is this area that is neglected the most. Yet it can have the largest overall impact on the extensibility, integrability, and usability of the application over time.

The temptation on the part of most development teams is to ignore the systems issues altogether early on in the project. The common rhetoric is that later on we will deal with them. What happens most of the time is that they are never dealt with or the sophisticated way in which they are addressed requires a major rewrite and rearchitecting of the overall knowledge-based application. It is strongly recommended that any development that is done should be performed in concert with a detailed understanding of the system requirements and their potential solutions. This will greatly reduce the overall time and cost to development of the knowledge-based application.

It is by the sophisticated and natural interweaving of procedural symbolic, heuristic, layered, and system-oriented tools that you can fully exploit the VAX computing architecture and its philosophy of computation. To do so is to take maximum advantage of what the VAX environment offers. Not to do so is to end up fighting and struggling at every turn to accomplish a meaningful result in a meaningful time frame.

9

Other Issues

Development and Delivery Environments

There are vast differences between an organization that is attempting to develop product for resale and one that is attempting to develop capability for internal consumption by its corporation. However, in both cases, it is necessary to understand intimately the application and system requirements that will be necessary to successfully build knowledge-based expert systems to address a particular problem. All too often these requirements are poorly understood or not understood at all. The temptation is to get the fastest computational environment and the flashiest knowledge engineering tool and then to proceed along the lines of rapid prototyping in the spirit of incremental knowledge engineering. This process usually leads to a false sense of security with great engineering efforts involved later on to produce the capability that has been researched and developed.

Strategy

The strategy for development and delivery stems from many years of experience in addressing vertical markets with real-world problems. It serves most organizations well to develop on the same environment that they are considering delivery on (see Figure 9-1). A common mis-

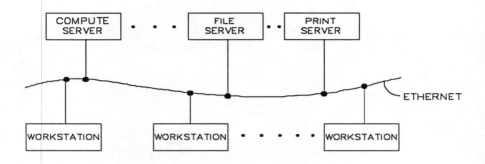

Figure 9-1   The development environment.

conception is the notion of ease of machine portability. That is, it is thought that it is easy to figure out later on what is required to deliver on an environment that is different from that which was used for development. In many cases this is not true. Moreover, this type of implementation is very engineering intensive in general. When you develop, it is important to identify up front all the system issues that will be required for delivery. It is strongly recommended that the development environment parallel in every aspect the delivery environment. Therefore, if a certain type of database connectivity or communications is necessary for delivery, these aspects should be a routine part of operational development in the development environment.

Delivering industrial-strength knowledge bases with a large degree of expertise requires using a platform intelligently in a way that tends to make much of the application specific to that platform. If you attempt to treat the VAX as a computing entity that is equally interchangeable with any other computing entity, vast opportunities will be lost, affecting both performance and functionality. Good LISP on a VAX, even if it is common LISP, is different than it is on another platform. The term "VAXification" of an application describes this process. To exploit a platform such as the VAX, along with its associated operating system VMS, requires an in-depth understanding of that environment.

Expert systems are very compute intensive and make excessive demands on systems' resources. These demands can be limited by the intelligent VAXification of any application or piece of code. For example, VMS as an operating system prefers a large collection of small processes rather than a small collection of large processes. Knowledge-based applications of the mid-to-large-scale range, if done in a vacuum, tend to be exceedingly large in nature. It is not impossible to build 100,000- or 200,000-page processes on the VAX; it is merely undesirable. Indeed, if you are attacking a very large application, you might have a physical limitation in terms of the size of a single knowledge-base process. However, the VAX has strong interprocess communication facilities. The best thing to do in the VAXification of an application is to break up an application into a multiprocess architecture, keeping the size of any given process down and using the very strong interprocess communication facilities that exist under VMS on the VAX. All too often expert systems that are designed for the VAX are designed as single-process computational architectures. This is in contrast to the intelligent use of the environment.

It is important to provide enough computes to allow effective development to ensue. There is nothing worse than telling a developer to go ahead and build a sophisticated expert system using a CPU-intensive heuristic tool without providing adequate compute resources for the job. Developers should have their own workstations that can be optimized to the type of development they are currently engaged in. In addition, the entire environment of all developers' workstations should be combined into a local area network that is integrated into one or more file servers, as well as one or more compute servers.

File servers are a convenient mechanism for storing away an ever-increasing history of development and capability. Compute servers can be necessary in the development environment if medium-to-large-scale applications are being attacked. It is very convenient to be able to ship a file or a subsystem over to a high-performance environment that is optimized for compiles in the development cycle. This seemingly high-end environment turns out in the long run to be the cost-effective way to do things. The people who are capable of architecting, designing, and implementing sophisticated knowledge-based applications are scarce and expensive. In the long run, providing a flexible and highly automated environment for development greatly reduces the overall cost of the operation.

It is important to have a test bed that exactly mimics the delivery environment. All too often expert systems that are no more than prototypes are delievered. There has not been extensive quality assurance (QA) nor have they been tested, verified, and validated in a production-oriented situation. All knowledge-based applications should undergo the same level of extensive in-house testing that any high-quality traditional application would. Unfortunately, this has not usually been the case. Many substandard knowledge-based systems have reached deployment only to expose needlessly flaws, bugs, and fundamental design errors.

In addition to a delivery test suite, the organization should be fully automated in terms of code management, source management, and documentation. The temptation on the part of most groups is to perform incremental knowledge engineering. This development environment more often than not leads to substandard delivery. If strict practices, standards, and automation are adopted early on, the group's overall productivity will greatly increase. Unfortunately, most AI organizations that exist today mimic more closely the university environment than the industrial environment. They inherit most of the failings of the university environment and usually little of the strengths. The university is not expected to produce industrial-strength software with finite resources and tough deadlines; the industrial environment is. In a proper development and delivery environment an AI organization should be mimicking very closely, with only subtle differences, traditional software engineering practices.

Laboratory versus Product Developments

If you are setting up a laboratory for research, the motivations and the environment should be different than if you are setting up an environment for product development or project work for a corporation. If the goal is a laboratory environment, it behooves the managers of that environment to organize it and staff it with as many tools, hardware platforms, and devices as is possible. Artificial intelligence is still an embryonic technology. There is much that awaits industrialization. A good laboratory is promulgated by a very broad mix of paradigms, computational environments, and programming resources. This is not a distraction; it is a catalyst in being able to do breakpath work.

However, if you are attempting to apply the technology that exists and to develop industrial-strength products, as well as projects, you are confronted with the need for specialization, standards, and focus. In the project environment, as well as in the product environment, it becomes critical to have an in-depth understanding of the tools and platforms that are going to be addressed. A mere surface understanding will not lead to industrial-strength results. All too often, in many industrial environments, the temptation is to own at least one of everything, to try at least one of everything. This attitude usually results in a hodge podge of capability, none of which can be VAXified in a meaningful sense. In the nonlaboratory environment, there should be a standard collection of tools, techniques, and methodologies, as well as an associated set of standards for their use. It will always be necessary to bring new technology into this type of environment. This is best served by having a special evaluation team that can routinely look at new technology, assess its worth to the organization, and then bring that technology into the mainstream under a very controlled set of circumstances.

This process will lead to better use of staff, as well as an evolutionary approach as opposed to an ad hoc revolutionary approach. Progress is very important. It is important that the evaluation procedures and methodologies for transference of new technology to the development staff is not overly cumbersome and that it is streamlined to allow the natural introduction of new technology. However, it is equally important that the developers are not continually bombarded by the ever-increasing proliferation of technology. As with all embryonic fields, the rate of growth at first is almost exponential. It is not uncommon that before a given organization has learned how to effectively use one LISP from one vendor, it is already off buying a second or a third LISP from other vendors. Having three LISPs in house without the knowledge of how to VAXify any of them does not serve the AI organization at any level.

Representation

The most fundamental requirement of building a knowledge-based application is choosing the appropriate representation for the various aspects of the problem. All computerized applications are made up of four fundamental components: control, data, representation, and application kernel logic.

Control is comprised of the information and procedure that implement the algorithm under which a solution will be obtained. Control is as important, if not more important, in a heuristic approach as it is in a purely traditional approach. Unless you carefully organize the declarative component of the knowledge base into knowledge classes and the procedural component of the logic base into rule sets and define a mechanism for scheduling the reasoning appropriately, you are going to build a very slow-moving system. The data is the actual values that are used for the reasoning purposes. Representation is the information and form associated with control logic, data, and application kernel logic. The application kernel logic is the actual collection of operators that can make a state transition in the solution to the problem.

It is key to note that knowledge representation includes all aspects of a declarative nature as well as of a procedural nature. The union of these two is the total representation of the problem. Schemas, objects, fact patterns, frames, as well as methods, rules, scripts, and demons, are all part of the knowledge representation of a problem. You have the opportunity to represent a given aspect of the application in many ways depending on what procedural, symbolic, heuristic, layered, or system software products you are using to build the application. The union of all the representation must embody a model for the underlying problem, as well as the algorithm that is necessary to find a solution to the problem.

All too often, in the representation for a particular problem not enough attention is given to detail. Sometimes there is too much of a burden placed on one form of representation and not enough placed on another form. When this happens, it usually leads to systems that are difficult to extend, debug, and, in general, maintain.

It is a good idea to keep the logic base as simple as possible and to place as much of the representation burden as possible on the declarative component. You should make the operators as simple and as obvious as possible, and the complexities of the problem, along with the algorithmic solution, should be transferred to the declarative component whenever possible. This results in a generally more maintainable, extensible, and understandable knowledge-based application.

By and large, rules that are compiled become unobservable logic to the rest of the application, whereas declarative representation is reasonable when you have to modify things not only at compile time but at run time as well. It is important to be able to allow the procedural component of the knowledge base to be as parametric and data driven as possible. By allowing values to be pattern matched or inherited as opposed to presumed, you can have a great deal of flexibility. Moreover, representation in the procedural components can also be data driven from the declarative component of the knowledge base. The proper parameterization and flexibility in the procedural component will set a firm foundation for the goals of learning, justification and explanation, verification and validation, maintenance, and reconfiguration on the fly.

The above is not in conflict with the goal of keeping the procedural component a collection of the simplest possible operators that will always allow a state transition to take place in the solution of the problem. Rather, it is an architectural, design, and implementation philosophy that will allow the procedural component to be driven in its representation and logic by the declarative component. If this is not done, the logic base becomes truly immutable, unable to reason about its existence or to modify itself at run time. By putting the maximum burden of representation, modeling, and problem solution on the declarative component and only applying the logical component as manifestations of that logic, you will set a firm foundation for an excellent knowledge-based application.

Control is a major issue in the architecture, design, and implementation of a knowledge-based application. Not only does it have to solve the problem of conflict resolution, but it is the control that is inherently responsible for arriving at a solution to the problem as efficiently as possible. Control should be explicit, not implicit. There should be specific, comprehensive, and complete declarative representation to support this requirement in the knowledge base. Moreover, the logic base that implements the focusing of attention and conflict resolution and the scheduling of the order of firing of rule sets should be data driven and able to accept parameters from the declarative component of the knowledge base.

The overall knowledge-base representation should be organized, explicit, and obvious. The topology, as well as the technology of the problem, should be represented declaratively. In general, you should not rely on any problem specifics to avoid the above guideline. Experience has shown that the ability to make a system increasingly more intelligent and able to reason about its own existence is directly correlated with the power and flexibility of the underlying representation. There are many ways to represent any given problem and there are very many paradigms of knowledge representation. Great attention to detail in the architecture, design, and implementation will elucidate the proper way to approach the problem. It is important to make sure that early on in the project you develop a clear set of goals for the knowledge representation and that these goals are continually sanity checked against the current design center, as well as against the implementation.

Learning

One of the great claims, as well as one of the potentials, of artificial intelligence is the ability to build systems that can learn. Although there have been some experimental attempts at capturing the essence of truly creative and independent learning, to date industrial manifestations have fallen far short of this lofty goal. There are many constructs that you can find in the literature to explain theoretical manifestations of learning. Most of them have yet to be applied in any real-world expert system application.

There are four methods by which you can get an expert system to at least simulate the characteristics of learning (see Figure 9-2). In general, these methodologies can be viewed more in line with the knowledge base being flexible, adaptable, and reconfigurable than being a true manifestation of creative independent thought. The four methodologies are as follows:

- Statistical
- Algorithmic
- Exploration
- Analogy

Most problems in the real world cannot be fully modeled by deterministic logic. Probabilities and statistical formulation are key to addressing many vertical market areas. An important technique to capture in a knowledge base is the ability to learn statistically in its declarative representation as well as in its procedural representation. The more the knowledge base runs, the better its own representation of random processes should be. Given the tools, techniques, and methodologies associated with symbolic and heuristic environments, this is a particularly natural thing to accomplish.

The obvious use of this construct is for the expert system to have the knowledge of statistical methods with a flexible representation to allow it to modify key parameters and distributions in an ongoing fashion. In addition to this, there is the ability for the expert system to be able to use fuzzy representation and fuzzy algorithms to solve the problem. It might not always be discernible that for any given in-

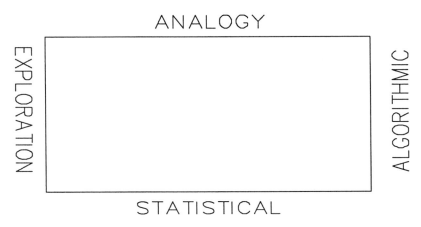

Figure 9-2 The building block of learning.

stance of a task what the best representation is or procedural logic should be. The expert system can modify its representation both declaratively and procedurally in a way so that it can apply knowledge based on a statistical understanding of benefit to the solution to the problem. This is important to understand and to use in applications that are not well formed. By doing this, the expert system can affect its control structure in terms of where it should be focusing its attention and how it should be attacking the problem in a manner that is most aligned with the current knowledge; it should also have a statistical understanding of how previous problems were successfully solved by the knowledge base.

All knowledge bases need an algorithm with which to solve the problem, even though this algorithm is usually not of a closed-form analytic nature. It is some subtle combination of traditional models and algorithms along with heuristic models and algorithms. However, there will be an algorithm. You need to know how and when you should start solving the problem, how to proceed along the solution to a problem, and when you are done and have arrived at an answer. If control is made explicit, as opposed to implicit, in the knowledge base and is properly supported by knowledge-class representation in the declarative component and rule set formulation in the procedural component, you have set the stage for the expert system to learn algorithmically, not only at the low level but at the high strategic level as well. For instance, if you are relying on some knowledge-intensive beam search to arrive at the solution to the problem, the width of the beam and the states that are chosen for expansion are candidates for the system to learn about algorithmically.

All too often, people cast in iron their algorithmic structures in the knowledge base. This defeats the very intent of symbolic and heuristic environments to be able to reconfigure themselves on the fly at both run time and compile time. At the low level, the knowledge base can learn algorithmically as well. If you adopt the techniques of using macros that are reconfigurable in a language like LISP, as well as rules that can write rules in the procedural component of the knowledge base, you can cast your algorithmic formulations at the low tactical level so that they are data driven based upon the experience of solving previous problems. This leads not only to a more intelligent solution to the problem, but it has the desirable benefit of usually generating a more compact and parsimonious representation and knowledge-base implementation.

Key to the ability to learn is an expert system's ability to explore alternatives. There are always time constraints in arriving at the solution to a problem. However, at any time there can be the "best guess method" that the expert system will use to efficiently kick out a solution. In concert with this, the expert system uses hypothetical reasoning to be able to explore better solution strategies to the problem that it was given. Based upon this exploration, the expert system should be able to modify itself in a statistical, as well as an algorithmic, sense to arrive at a more efficient and desirable answer the next time. Moreover, there are always times when the expert system will not be fully loaded in terms of solving a live task. This could happen at off hours as well as during the normal operational cycle.

An important way for the expert system to learn is to be able to reevaluate past problems by increasing the exploration associated with solving them. In order to codify a new desirable methodology, it is important to characterize the solution process in terms of a set of metrics for rank evaluation purposes. Such metrics might be timed to solution, number of computes, confidence factor in the solution, system resources consumed, and the like. If you architect, design, and implement the knowledge base to allow for an incremental mode of exploration with a subsequent update of the algorithmic structure, you have gone very far toward capturing the essence of learning.

Analogy is a very obvious technique to accomplish the spirit of learning in a knowledge base. Simply put, the expert system should be able to catalog possible instances of the problem which it was designed to solve. These instances of the problem should be represented along with attributes that clearly delineate important key characteristics. The algorithmic solution to the problem should contain a component that looks to match up characteristics of a particular instance of a problem with an optimized solution methodology. If you develop a system along these lines, you can incrementally make the knowledge base more intelligent by teaching it more analogies. Moreover, there usually is a central tendency to the solution of any problem. This central tendency might tend to solve 70, 80, or 90 percent of the particular problem instances that might be confronted. However, with all real-world problems, there are always boundary cases that are not adequately solved by the central tendency. Describing these boundary cases intelligently and learning about new ones by analogy can lead an expert system to incrementally refine its precision in handling all cases in the problem under discussion.

A key insight architecturally to implement learning is the ability to couple intimately and subtly a stable storage architecture with an in-memory knowledge base. Learning requires more often than not large amounts of representation and data and a place to be able to dynamically save state and computation. You are well served if learning is a key requirement or goal of the knowledge-based application to integrate tightly a product such as Digital's relational database with any heuristic or symbolic tool or tools in which you might choose to build the application. It should be quite obvious that if analytical analogy methods are used, this becomes totally impractical very quickly unless a stable storage architecture is present.

Justification and Explanation

Like learning, a major claim of expert systems technology is its ability to justify and explain its thought processes at arriving at an intelligent solution. By and large, like learning, the industrial reality has fallen far short of the theoretical foundations. In addressing vertical market applications in the process, general manufacturing, graphic arts, and government arenas, a free-form totally asynchronous unanticipated justification and explanation facility is not required. What is required is the ability to anticipate, from the viewpoint of the application, those key questions and key reports that you might ask during the solution of a particular problem.

In order to build a sufficient and elegant justification and explanation facility it is necessary to ascertain during the knowledge acquisition process exactly the set of required queries and under what set of circumstances they would be used to support live production use of the knowledge base. The best method for building a justification and explanation facility is to anticipate beforehand exactly what is necessary and then design a declarative knowledge set that comprises the declarative representation in a knowledge class to answer those questions. In addition, it will be necessary to construct a justification and explanation rule set to service the queries. At any point, based upon execution to the solution of the problem, the rule set that is associated with justification and explanation is depositing in the justification and explanation knowledge class the answers to the supported reports and queries. It is highly desirable in justification and explanation for medium-to-large-scale systems to rely upon a stable storage architecture to actually deliver the explanations. In most systems, all live queries, as well as justification and explanations, are actually retrieved out of the stable storage architecture rather than the live-in memory knowledge base as is commonplace today.

It is anticipating clearly what the real requirements of a justification and explanation facility are in the live production use of the system that leads to the necessary simplifications in order to successfully implement an industrial-strength facility. For instance, if you are building a knowledge base to optimize a particular process, you should anticipate up front the queries that are necessary to support its use. Such queries might be: Why did you choose that particular strategy? What were the alternatives to the optimization methodology that you used? Questions like these can then be mapped architecturally into the overall knowledge-base structure in a way that can be supported and implemented by current technology and understanding.

High Availability

Depending upon the market and the vertical application being addressed, there might or might not be a high availability and/or fault-tolerant requirement for the expert system. If these are requirements, the techniques and methodologies associated with distributed AI become important. A simple way to accomplish high availability is to allow for the stable storage architecture to be shadowed either logically or physically on one or more machines. Doing this sets the foundation for easy recovery. If this is not satisfactory, a truly transaction-oriented paradigm coupling multiple computers with multiple stable storage architectures and in-memory knowledge bases becomes necessary. DEC provides a number of outstanding tools and facilities that allow you to accomplish high availability in a cost-effective manner without years of development. In addition, there are some third-party software firms that have meaningful facilities in this area as well. By the appropriate architecture, design, and implementation of DECnet facilities, Rdb, cluster technology, and software like ACMS, you can accomplish in a straightforward manner a nice environment that will have adequate fail-soft characteristics.

Nonstop AI requires additional system-level services of a check-pointing and save-state nature. These two can be accomplished on the VAX, but they require great attention to system-level detail in design and in implementation.

If you have a high-availability or fail-soft requirement, by using the techniques of integrated artificial intelligence and distributed AI in conjunction with a cooperating expert system design, you can naturally accomplish any level of survivability on the VAX.

Verification and Validation

Given the nature of most knowledge-based applications, it becomes increasingly important to verify and validate the system at all phases of development as well as in actual production use (see Figure 9-3). These systems tend to be more complex to debug and more susceptible to subtle errors. The design should include as many error handlers and live verifiers and validators as is possible. In a knowledge-based application, you should attempt to trap as early as possible any and all erroneous inputs, computations, or outputs in the actual production process.

Moreover, a knowledge base should undergo extensive QA before its release. Traditionally, this is accomplished by letting the domain expert interact with the application, thereby critiquing its decision-making process. This is a valuable methodology but one that is of an ad hoc nature. The construction of a verification and validation test suite becomes a very important entity in the delivery of a product or project. This test suite should be capable of exercising the knowledge base automatically against a broad collection of instances of the problem being solved. In addition, a feature of the knowledge base should be the capability, in the delivered system, to build additional test cases for the customer. This is important so that when a new

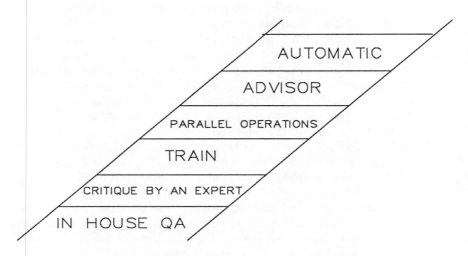

Figure 9-3   The verification and validation ladder.

release of software occurs, the customer can run an instance problem test case against the new version of the knowledge base and can also test cases that were run by the vendor or by the internal development group.

In general, for most applications, with a little thought and design, you can generate an orthogonal collection of tests that will exercise the majority of dimensions of the problem-solving capability of the knowledge base. Very rarely in knowledge-base application development and delivery is enough attention paid to detail in the area of verification and validation. It is important in the verification and validation of a knowledge-based application to have a methodology for introducing it into the live production environment. First, it should undergo as extensive quality assurance as possible against the development test suite. After this has been successfully accomplished, the system should be brought into the production environment and first used in a training mode to allow the operators of the system to learn how to use it and to also expose any other inadequacies and problems with it. After the successful conclusion of the training phase, the system should then be used in a parallel mode of operation with the existing methodology for handling the problem. This would be essentially using it as an advisor and not allowing it to close any loops automatically even if this is part of the design center of the functionality. Upon successful conclusion of this phase, operations can be switched over and the old methodology discontinued.

If the system is geared to being an advisor, this is the final step in the process. However, if the system is geared to making some automatic decisions and closing some communication paths, control paths, and data paths dynamically on its own, the system should be run in the advisor mode until complete confidence is gained. Finally, the system should be allowed to close the loop and automatically take action if this is part of its design center. The system should be designed so that at any time it could be easily and conveniently backed out from its mode of operation to one of less severity and import to the organization. Appropriate functions should be implemented in the application to be able to naturally and intelligently support these many levels of verification and validation. Suffice it say that a phased implementation approach is absolutely necessary, and the appropriate facilities to stage the knowledge base from its inception in the development environment to its live production use in an automatic sense should be fully anticipated and supported early on in the project or product development.

10

Applications

Overview

In most of the significant vertical markets there exists great interest and activity in using artificial intelligence and expert systems to address tough state of the art problems that are industry specific. Addressing these problems requires not only deep-seated knowledge of computer science and artificial intelligence but extensive domain knowledge as well. More often than not, these problems have existed for a number of years. Organizations have either failed in their attempts to automate solutions or have arrived at solutions that are considered unsatisfactory and that only capture a small fraction of the potential return on investment that an adequate solution to the problem area would generate.

To address these problems requires a very practical and level-headed attitude along with the ability to appropriately apply state of the art technology. The tools, techniques, and methodologies associated with integrated artificial intelligence, cooperating expert systems, distributed artificial intelligence, domain-specific solution shells, and time-critical AI have been found to be central to their intelligent solution. Moreover, a general paradigm of reasoning has been identified as a pervasive model for many vertical market applications.

This model of reasoning is called the intelligent reasoning cycle (see Figure 10-1). There are four phases to it. The first phase is the

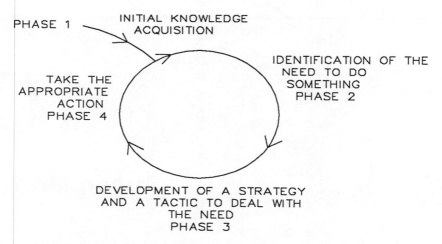

Figure 10-1 The intelligent reasoning cycle.

knowledge acquisition phase. In this phase, the domain-specific solution shell arrives at a particular site. Forms, questions, and other mechanisms are used to elucidate the site-specific information. This is usually comprised of the site-specific configuration, data structures, goals, rules, and key parameter values. Once the knowledge acquisition phase is completed, the system is capable of entering the intelligent reasoning cycle. This cycle is intended to be event driven and asynchronous in nature.

In the second phase of the cycle, the knowledge-based application is attempting to identify the need to do something. It is a waste of computes to always have the knowledge base reasoning. The knowledge base should be event driven and capable of focusing its attention given the state of the problem solution and what is taking place in the problem environment at large. If the problem at hand is scheduling, in this phase the knowledge base is attempting to identify the need to schedule. This might be done through a combination of diagnostics or experiments that the knowledge base conducts in a live environment or in a reactive sense in which the knowledge base is merely analyzing information that is presented to it.

Upon completion of this phase, the knowledge base either has or has not identified the need to do something and the attributes and characteristics of the problem. If it has identified the need to do something, the knowledge base would enter the third phase of operation. In this phase the knowledge base would develop a strategy and a tactic to deal with the problem that was elucidated in the identification phase. In the intelligent reasoning cycle, the underpinning can be viewed, in an intellectual sense, as a knowledge base comprised of a number of fundamental techniques for a specific domain. In the scheduling example, you might have methodologies that will generate a new master schedule or methodologies that will merely refine a piece of an existing schedule. Moreover, there can be scheduling techniques that are good in a deterministic environment as opposed to scheduling techniques that generate a better solution for a stochastic environment.

In phase 3, the knowledge base will take the problem that was identified in phase 2 and analyze it against its knowledge base of methodologies to address the particular domain area. It is important that in this phase the knowledge base is capable of developing strategies and tactics that are hybrids and combinations of any fundamental techniques that are modeled. More often than not the intelligent solution to the problem is not any one simple orthogonal methodology but rather a hybrid of fundamental techniques. At the completion of the third phase in the intelligent reasoning cycle, the knowledge base has formulated the strategy and the tactic to deal with the problem and its attributes that were identified in phase 2.

In phase 4 of the intelligent reasoning cycle, the knowledge-based application will take the appropriate action based upon the strategy and tactic that was formulated in phase 3. It is important to understand that this intelligent reasoning cycle is not a purely cyclic sequential loop. Identification of the need to do something can be taking place while the knowledge base is taking action on a previous problem. The intelligent reasoning cycle is meant to convey a topology as opposed to a definitive sequence of reasoning.

The system should be architected, designed, and implemented so that knowledge acquisition can be done at any time. The initial knowledge acquisition provides the initial condition for the application to begin the intelligent reasoning cycle. However, like all applications, it will have to go through various adjustments, tuning, and changes because of environmental upsets. Such upsets might be comprised of changes in operational requirements, configurations, goals, and the like.

Architecturally, you should view the implementation of the intelligent reasoning cycle as being made up of a number of concentric layered systems. The inner system represents a high-performance, fully configured run-time kernel that is always capable of taking time-critical action based on the current best estimate of the things to do given the current environment. The outer layer is made up of an intelligent reasoning component that is attempting to figure out how to modify the run-time kernel.

There are other models of reasoning besides the intelligent reasoning cycle. However, for the vertical markets that will be addressed in this chapter, it has been found to be a highly useful architectural format. Its spirit is one that is in line with time criticalness and online applications. Its intent is to provide a knowledge-based environment that is capable of keeping up with the state transition changes in the real world.

It is important to note that the knowledge acquisition phase that has to be performed initially, and that could be performed at any other time, should require no computer science or artificial intelligence knowledge. Historically, the best-received knowledge-based applications have been the ones with which end users who only knew their problem domain were comfortable with right away. If artificial intelligence and expert systems are to gain broad industrial acceptance in a live production mode, easy-to-use applications that are generic in nature but can be easily made specific are a must.

Process Control

One of the largest vertical market areas is commonly referred to as the process control industries. This marketplace is comprised of such segments as:

- Petrochemical
- Chemical
- Pharmaceutical
- Food and beverage
- Pulp and paper
- Glass
- Rubber and plastics
- Metals
- Discrete manufacturing

In all of the above industries, you are confronted with automating a process, which might be a combination of a number of subprocesses,

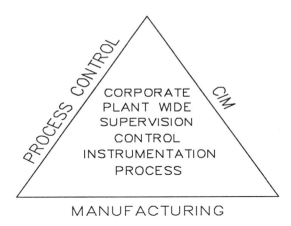

Figure 10-2 The automation pyramid.

that needs to be controlled. In the plant environment, there are a number of levels necessary to address this function (see Figure 10-2).

At the lowest level, there are instruments that monitor, sense, and manipulate process variables. These instruments are then interconnected to a control structure that is capable of implementing a control law. Typical industrial-strength control structures might be realized on such devices as single-loop instruments, programmable logic controllers, and distributed control systems. All of these controllers implement some combination of feed forward and feedback control technology.

At the next level is the supervisory host computer. This computer is usually interconnected to the control hardware via some sort of gateway or network communications. The supervisory host maintains the databases and the applications that would sit up top of the primary control function. In most plant environments this supervisory host is interconnected via another communication path to a plantwide computer system that is maintaining the business and overall manufacturing aspects of the plant. Finally, this plantwide system is interconnected into a corporate computing system that will run the corporatewide applications.

There are many opportunities for introducing artificial intelligence and expert systems into process control. Most of these opportunities are best realized by implementing the functionality on the supervisory host computer that is tightly interconnected into the control layer. Examples of important and pervasive application areas that are ideal candidates for the building of intelligent software for the process control industries are as follows:

- Computer-aided instruction
- Alarm management
- Scheduling
- Maintenance
- Configuration
- Statistical process control and quality assurance
- Tuning
- Supervisory control and optimization
- Simulation
- Plant planning and optimization
- Batch operator decision support

All of these application areas are pervasive in the sense that there are some 50,000 raw materials processing plants in the United States and, to a greater or lesser degree, they are all confronted with the same types of problems. By architecting, designing, and implementing a domain-specific solution shell, you can meaningfully address a large collection of these problems in a natural and easy-to-install manner.

Intelligent Tuning

An example will illustrate the above concept. Let us look at the problem of intelligent tuning. Most of the control function implemented at the control layer realizes some form of proportional, integral, and derivative control (see Figure 9-3). This control law requires three coefficients to be properly specified for the right functionality to take place. These coefficients are the constants of proportionality, integration, and differentiation of the error signal. If in a given plant there is a distributed control system that is tied into the process through a collection of instruments that implements 100 PID control loops, there are 300 parameters that need to be appropriately set for adequate performance in the plant environment to take place. This performance is a measure of throughput, product quality, profitability, minimization of the variance of the product quality, cost of production, and the like.

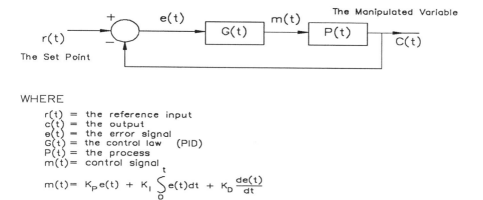

WHERE

$r(t)$ = the reference input
$c(t)$ = the output
$e(t)$ = the error signal
$G(t)$ = the control law   (PID)
$P(t)$ = the process
$m(t)$ = control signal

$$m(t) = K_P e(t) + K_I \int_0^t e(t)dt + K_D \frac{de(t)}{dt}$$

Figure 10-3   A simple single-input single-output PID process control loop.

Assessing these parameters at any point is not a trivial process; it is one that is presently very labor and knowledge intensive. Moreover, the values of these parameters are dependent on the state of the process that is being controlled, as well as on the feedstocks that are used for manufacture and, of course, the particular product that is being manufactured. By and large, the values of the PID coefficients in all the loops need to be tuned or adjusted relatively frequently to result in an optimal control structure for the plant environment.

Presently, this represents an unautomated opportunity. By and large, in most plant environments, you can find a majority of the control loops that are suboptimally tuned with the resultant economic consequences for the operation. The opportunity for knowledge-based systems is to build an expert plantwide tuning system that would reside on a host supervisory computer. This expert system would be tightly integrated with the control layer to allow both data and effect to be easily interchanged in a timely fashion. The expert system would have three fundamental tasks.

The first task would be the identification of the need to tune. Not all loops need to be parameterically optimized all the time. The expert system would be capable of inserting diagnostics into the environment to measure the quality of goodness of control. It would have the capability of reasoning both in the time domain and the frequency domain to identify problems. Given that the expert system identified the need to tune a particular control structure, in the second task the expert system would have to develop a strategy and a tactic for tuning the suboptimal loop.

There are many techniques for solving the tuning problem: techniques that are good for set-point disturbances, techniques that are good for load disturbances, and techniques that are optimal when you analyze the problem in the time domain as opposed to the frequency domain. Moreover, stochastic noise entering the process or control structure represents a fundamentally different tuning problem from all the above. The different ways of adaptively tuning a control structure based upon the state of the process, the control technology and topology that is implemented, the goals of goodness of tuning, and the nature and intensity of the disturbances vary greatly.

In the second task, the expert system will need to develop a tactic and a strategy to deal with the problem that was identified in the first task. It is important in task 1 of the intelligent reasoning cycle that not only is a problem identified but that its characteristics, attributes, and general environmental state are elucidated. This information is used by the knowledge base in task 2 of the intelligent reasoning cycle to choose the appropriate tuning technique from a knowledge base that contains many. Indeed, the technique might be a hybrid of a number of fundamental orthogonal techniques, each of which addresses a piece of the problem that was identified in task 1. Finally, in task 3 of the intelligent reasoning cycle, the knowledge base takes the appropriate action and inserts in a bumpless transition fashion the new optimal tuning coefficients into the distributed control law that is being implemented by the control hardware.

Building a heuristic plantwide tuning system for traditional control laws in the processing industries is an important application area. Purely traditional approaches will fail because of their inflexibility and because of the fact that essentially this knowledge-based application is solving in a time-critical fashion a very high-order parametric optimization problem. Only by the use of intelligent integrated artificial intelligence techniques can you hope to reduce the problem to manageable dimensions, thereby keeping up with the demands of the actual process environment. It is important that the knowledge base be able to intelligently focus its attention to effectively use compute resources at any point during the intelligent reasoning cycle.

The knowledge-based application might reason as follows to focus its attention. The highest priority is dealing with any observed instability. If an instability is detected, the knowledge base should immediately tune the associated control structure. The next priority would be to make use of any exogenous or indigenous disturbances. This represents a free diagnostic in the identification of the need to tune task and does not require the knowledge base to introduce through the control system an artificial diagnostic to elucidate the state of tuning for a particular control structure. Finally, if there are no instabilities and no exogenous disturbances, each control structure should be looked at according to an algorithm such as last time tuned.

It should be obvious that the knowledge base will be doing multiple tasks at the same time. The number of tasks depends upon the size of the computer that is being used, the number of loops in the plant that need to be intelligently tuned, the underlying time constants of the various process elements, and the control structures and disturbances.

The VAX, with its very strong communications and layered software products, presents an ideal platform on which to build a heuristic plantwide tuning system that can be naturally integrated into control system products. The VAX is already widely accepted in the process industries as an excellent choice for a supervisory host computer. It is at this level in the plant on which the intelligent tuning system should function.

It will be important to develop a flexible and easy-to-use interface and, in particular, a knowledge acquisition paradigm. When the domain-specific solution shell arrives at a particular plant, those responsible for the control of the process will need to interact with it to make it site specific. In the case of a tuning expert system, the following types of knowledge will need to be specified on a site-specific basis:

• Control technology
• Control topology
• Process technology
• Process topology
• Goodness of tuning
• Configuration
• Product quality and variation

It is key for it to be possible for the site-specific knowledge necessary to be acquired without any need for computer science or artificial intelligence.

The tuning problem is pervasive in the process industries. By and large, if you visit a plant and do a control system audit, you will find many loops that are maltuned, directly affecting the quality of the product and the overall manufacturing process. Only by the use of integrated artificial intelligence, cooperating expert systems, distributed artificial intelligence, domain-specific solution shell, and time-critical AI technology can you hope to arrive at a natural, easy-to-use, and sufficient solution to the types of problems in the process industries.

Intelligent Simulation

Traditional simulations and simulation environments are characterized by their inflexibility and lack of specific domain knowledge with respect to a particular problem. Even the traditional simulation environments that are easier to use, in the sense that they attempt to minimize the amount of computer science and programming necessary, still require a high degree of customization and procedural programming to fulfill the requirements of any real-world problems. Moreover, they are not easy to modify and enhance because the parametric structure of the simulation methodologies are represented as compiled logic to the simulation shell's data structures. The area of intelligent simulations (ISIM) represents a vast industrial opportunity in the process and general manufacturing industries that the VAX is ideally suited to address.

Characteristics

There are many desirable characteristics associated with building an intelligent simulation for any industrial processes. First, by using advanced artificial intelligence and expert system techniques to develop the structure of the declarative components of the knowledge base, you can provide an environment that is very easy to install and modify by noncomputer science or AI people. Second, the underlying simulation methods and modeling techniques can be data driven in a parametric sense from the declarative component of the knowledge base. This means that by changing any of the attributes or objects that are undergoing simulation, the resultant optimal simulation procedures will automatically be configured and used. This removes the need for either modification of the procedural code or running a suboptimal simulation.

An important characteristic of an intelligent simulation is its intimate knowledge about the domain. For the user to be able to install, use, modify, or apply it intelligently, it would not be necessary to know anything more than domain logic as opposed to intimate deep-seated computer science and artificial intelligence. The knowledge base would exploit heuristic and procedural simulation methods. This is an important characteristic of the ISIM because not all of the underlying physics can usually be captured, modeled, or computed using purely closed-form analytic representation.

An intelligent simulation environment is capable of being used in a number of different modes of operation. The following examples of use stem from the process and general manufacturing industries.

Training

In this mode, people would be able to gain experience with actually operating the process without having to manipulate real process environments. An intelligent simulator is ideally qualified to be an intelligent trainer. The justification and explanation facilities in the knowledge base in conjunction with the overall interactive nature of the environment makes this activity a natural mode of use.

Design

In addition to training, an intelligent simulation environment understands and knows the physics of the domain being simulated. It allows for rapid exploration of alternatives to the current process technology and topology, as well as to the surrounding control technology and topology. It, therefore, provides an ideal environment to use as an intelligent design tool that is able to analyze process and control alternatives to meet management objectives. Fundamentally, understanding how a process behaves and its underlying physics is key to the manufacturing environment as well as to the necessities of control to accomplish objectives. The simulation environment will allow process and control research to be conducted in a cost-effective and nondestructive fashion.

Planning

You can use the intelligent simulation environment to plan new operational procedures and methodologies for the manufacturing environment. These planning experiments should lead to new standards that streamline operations for a particular industrial process.

Control

In order to develop control strategies that provide the necessary return and characteristic benefits that are desired, it is necessary to have an exploratory environment in which to develop and test them. An intelligent simulation of an industrial process would provide such a mechanism, allowing you to develop the associated control strategies that would be necessary to improve overall profitability and performance.

In-Plant Decision Support

If the intelligent simulation is designed with the capability for a fast-forward mode of operation supporting asynchronous events, it could be used as an intelligent in-plant decision support tool to be able to support the operators in the live manufacturing process. Characteristically, if at any point a plant operator can ask the simulation to look forward 1, 2, or X hours, you have a very good system to be able to optimize the present strategies to be most in line with future forecasts and requirements.

Technical Direction

Fundamental to the approach will be the construction of a knowledge base that will use many state of the art artificial intelligence and expert system approaches and tightly integrated traditional logic. The ISIM should rely on an object-oriented inheritance mechanism with a generic taxonomy for a particular industrial process in order to be able to describe the declarative component of the knowledge base. This will allow structuring the overall industrial problem in a form that makes it easy to modify, extend, and field install. Such modifications might encompass further depth in the knowledge about the particular industrial process as well as encompassing other processes that you desire to have simulated. The operation of installing the ISIM in a particular plant environment will merely require filling out the set of instances for that particular plant. This can be done without any computer science or artificial intelligence knowledge.

A tightly integrated and highly efficient procedural component of the knowledge base that will make use of the object-oriented inheritance component of the declarative base is an absolute necessity.

Other Characteristics of the Simulation

The ISIM should be event driven and should allow the support of asynchronous logic to take place. It should contain a justification and explanation facility and a reporting facility. No specific LISP knowledge or AI knowledge or indeed detailed computer science should be necessary for the routine use of the ISIM within its current design center for a particular industrial process. The simulation should include the provision for dummy objects, relationships, and attributes that can be specified without previously anticipated physics being implied.

Performance Requirements

The metric of performance should be based upon how fast the ISIM can simulate fast forward relative to process time. It should be determined how fast the simulation needs to be in fast-forward mode early on. This mode of the system should be adjustable and selectable for any given simulation run or environment spanning slow down, normal process time, and fast forward.

The VAX, with its excellent layered software products, provides an ideal environment in which to build a generic intelligent simulation environment. The VAX is capable of building domain-specific shells in a highly integrated fashion. The ISIM is a tangible example of a domain-specific shell. It requires the integration of traditional databases, communications, and user interface technologies that are already available off the shelf. In addition, the ISIM will most likely be used as one of a number of cooperating expert systems in which time criticalness and distribution are important. Because of the range of processors that are currently available and Digital's strong networking and communications tools, all of the above becomes possible in a cost-effective development cycle when it is attempted on the current VAX system.

Computer-Integrated Manufacturing

CIM is a technology and a concept that is very important to the process industries as well as to the general manufacturing industries at large. Its goal is to be able to integrate in an intelligent fashion both hierarchically and latitudinally information, control, process, and analysis extending up from the single process, throughout the plant, and into the corporation. It is characterized by requirements that can only be fulfilled by the key important AI technologies that have been described above. Problem areas that are particularly important and are natural applications for intelligent software follow:

• Computer-aided design
• Order entry
• Inventory control
• Database management
• Scheduling
• Maintenance

When bringing new technology into a live operation, it is always necessary to integrate. Given the goals of CIM, integrated artificial intelligence and distributed artificial intelligence become key technologies. It is important in this environment to also recognize the need for an intelligent supervisor that would provide functionality above and beyond that of a mere intelligent operating system to an application.

It is obvious from the previous section on process control that the need and the requirement for cooperating expert systems is strong. This requirement is carried forward into the CIM environment. However, at this level, you are going to be confronted with the management of many intelligent applications. This logic is best served by another knowledge base that can provide the various control, coordination, and operational interchanges that will be necessary to make the entire collection of intelligent knowledge bases seem cognitive and synchronized. This requirement will be even more severe and will require even more functionality than what is commonly provided by the normal cooperating expert system environment that was described earlier.

In both process control and computer integrated manufacturing, time-critical AI is of great concern. If a loop in a plant becomes unstable or a feedstock gets contaminated, making an absolutely brilliant decision too late is of absolutely no value. Constantly arbitrating between timeliness versus intelligence is an absolute requirement in computer-integrated manufacturing and process control. Explicit modeling of the underlying dynamics and time constants with intelligent constraint reasoning will be absolutely necessary.

A key application area will be the architecture, design, and implementation of intelligent database facilities to support the lofty goals of CIM. These intelligent database facilities should allow a knowledge base to support the following activities:

* Database design
* Database connectivity
* Application generation
* Query optimization
* Data management and modeling
* Performance analysis and tuning

Given the current trends and standardizations in database technology, it will be particularly natural and optimal to support SQL as a standard in building intelligent database facilities for the CIM environment. At its heart, much of CIM represents a real-time database environment with a set of supervisory applications built on top of that layer. Artificial intelligence and expert systems are ideally suited not only to address some of the applications but to provide the overall management coordination and facilities associated with CIM down through the layers to direct process control.

Intelligent Scheduling

Intelligent scheduling is a key component in building an overall intelligent computer-integrated manufacturing environment (see Figure 10-4). It is very representative in its characteristics and goals of any ICIM application.

The development of a flexible knowledge-based scheduling application should be easy for the user to configure without having

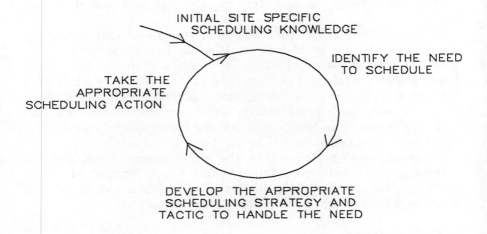

INITIAL SITE SPECIFIC
SCHEDULING KNOWLEDGE

IDENTIFY THE NEED
TO SCHEDULE

TAKE THE
APPROPRIATE
SCHEDULING ACTION

DEVELOP THE APPROPRIATE
SCHEDULING STRATEGY AND
TACTIC TO HANDLE THE NEED

Figure 10-4   The intelligent reasoning cyle for scheduling.

knowledge of computer science or artificial intelligence. This scheduling application should be able to address the problems in the continuous, semicontinuous, and batch processing industries. The scheduling application would use the concepts and techniques of integrated artificial intelligence. Namely the system would include knowledge of many traditional techniques such as linear programming, PERT, CPM, just in time (JIT), and MRP in its knowledge base. In addition it would have true heuristic knowledge surrounding these traditional approaches to extend their accuracy and functionality in the plant environment. A scheduling system such as this would be able to provide benefits to the plant in the following areas:

- Maximization of throughput and yields
- Resource analysis and scheduling (people, tools, and components)
- Bottleneck analysis and capacity planning (floating and fixed)
- Maximizing of the number of batches though a facility
- Reduction of operator burden
- Ability to run the entire scheduling system in fast forward (detailed prediction, forecasting, and simulation) in order to help perform operator decision support, especially in the batch environment areas
- Facilities and inventory planning
- Area set-up optimizations

- Handling of assemblies
- Alternate routings
- Machine maintenance schedules

Existing scheduling systems generally use deterministic methods that optimize on a very limited set of factors, such as due dates, work in process levels, and machine use. These systems fail to model many relevant scheduling considerations such as:

- Activities that require multiple resources.
- Alternate activity networks. Most existing systems handle only alternate work centers for a specific activity.
- Preference among work centers when alternate manufacturing methods are possible. Alternate methods often vary widely in cost.
- Personnel.
- Tooling.
- Raw and component materials required for an activity. Modeling materials by order may cause delivery earlier than necessary and cannot reflect alternate materials that require different manufacturing.
- Preferred customers.
- Storage space in and between work centers.
- Interorder relationships.
- Stochastic variances in activity times.
- Subcontract options for activities or orders.
- Assemblies.
- Conditional, relaxable constraints. When modeled at all, constraints are absolute (typically a date restriction on an activity).
- Management objectives and policies.
- Production and financial quotas.
- Due date importance and acceptable variance by order or order class. An emergency order has far less acceptable variance than an order build for inventory. Priorities do not model this well.
- Stability constraints. Existing systems recompute the schedule without reference to the prior schedule. The resulting schedule changes often disrupt support activity based on the old schedule.

The modeling is usually a reflection of the internal methodology of the scheduling system. If the models were extended to include some of the items above, the deterministic methods used would cause exponentially increasing run times. Moreover, most existing systems lack a good interactive scheduling interface and are difficult to interface with other systems.

In addition to integrated artificial intelligence, this scheduling system should rely very heavily on other methodologies including cooperating expert systems, distributed artificial intelligence, and time-critical AI. The system should be built so that it is easy to install in a live plant and maintainable by the existing plant personnel.

Computer-integrated manufacturing represents a vast opportunity, especially in the process industries. An important requirement that the system should meet is to intelligently schedule in a real-time online mode. Purely numerical approaches can lead to horrendously large computations and models that are cumbersome when severe time constraints are part of the problem. Historically, scheduling has been done according to purely numerical approaches, such as linear programming, when a computer is involved. Even with this restrictive modeling approach, great success and benefits have been derived to date through automation of the scheduling problem. However, this approach is inflexible and can only handle the limited number of objectives and goals that could be determined a priori in a static sense.

The proposed CIM application should be built as a domain-dependent solution shell, integrating traditional and heuristic techniques. By having true expert capability interacting with, using, and manipulating the more traditional numerical approaches, the system will more intelligently reason about dynamic scheduling issues in a timely manner.

This expert scheduling system should be capable of operating in a number of modes of operation. One mode is the interactive mode, which represents on-demand intelligent scheduling. In this mode a human being would ask the expert scheduling system to go ahead and produce a new optimal schedule given the current environment and goals. A second mode would be the automatic mode, in which the expert scheduling system would be constantly looking to identify the need to schedule. If it identified the need to schedule, the system would then select an appropriate scheduling method given site-specific goals, objectives, and the current plant state and then would go ahead and schedule the facility. In order to have a successful automatic mode it is necessary to construct a knowledge base that is rich in its generic approaches to scheduling.

The site-specific customization in the field would be accomplished by a plant-knowledgeable person or persons through the use of simple forms, answers to questions, and a graphics-drawing facility. The site-specific knowledge necessary in order for the scheduling system to make intelligent choices would be resident in the knowledge base as a result of this easy field installation process.

The knowledge base would provide expert functionality in the following areas:

- Identification of the need to schedule
- Determination of which scheduling techniques to employ
- Intelligent model construction and enhancement
- Intelligent constraint identification, enhancement, and relaxation
- Generation of goals and subgoals for its focus of attention
- Intelligent forecasting, simulation, and prediction

In addition, the knowledge base would contain the following knowledge classes in its declarative component:

- Scheduling techniques
- Scheduling goals and objectives
- Plant technology
- Plant topology
- Item topology
- Item technology
- Time constraints
- Item constraints
- Plant constraints
- Resource constraints (material, personnel, machine, processes)
- Customer preferences
- Time model (overtime, shifts, holidays)
- Preference classes
- Classes of resources (expendable, reusable)
- Statistical variations of process time
- World model
- Optimization methods
- Site specifics
- Learning
- Justification and explanation
- Meta knowledge
- Metrics on the quality of a schedule
- Stochastic processes

The logic base component of the knowledge base would contain the following rule sets:

- Declarative agenda control
- Directed knowledge-oriented search strategies
- Scheduling techniques
- Scheduling goals and objectives
- Plant topology
- Plant technology
- Item topology
- Item technology
- Time constraints
- Resource constraints (material, personnel, machines, processes)
- Metrics on the quality of a schedule
- Plant constraints
- Item constraints
- Stochastic processes
- World model
- Optimization methods
- Site specifics
- Learning
- Justification and explanation
- Meta knowledge
- Customer preferences
- Time model (overtime, shifts, holidays)
- Preference classes
- Classes of resources (expendable, reusable)
- Statistical variations of process time

This knowledge-based scheduling application should be architected, designed, and implemented to be easily integrated in an online, real-time sense into the existing MIS, CAD, CAM, and CIM computing environments in a plant.

Intelligent gateways and interfaces should be provided for existing applications, databases, communications, and computing environments on both the plant and corporate levels. A stable storage architecture with networking facilities would be integral to the system to facilitate distributed AI, high availability, and fault-tolerant AI. The entire application environment should be built on a symbolic transaction processing model (STPM). This STPM should implement a symbolic client server paradigm with a data flow model of computation. Cooperating expert system technology would be key to the application architecture, design, and implementation. This will allow the system to handle multiple distributed plant sites, tightly integrated with corporate decision-making capability and automation.

A knowledge-based scheduling application, such as the one above, would be ideal on Digital's VAX computing line, making extensive use of Digital's layered software, networking, and communications products. The above proposed ICIM application is feasible given today's VAX-based tools and techniques.

Government

The military and other associated government agencies represent another vast area for the development of knowledge-based applications using the appropriate technologies that best accomplish the requirements of that environment. It is important in this area not to lose sight of the fact that the standard approved Department of Defense languages are Ada and common LISP. This area of application is characterized by the needs and requirements of the following functional areas of the government:

- The various military establishments
- The scientific agencies
- The intelligence agencies

Almost every possible problem that you could envision is routinely encountered in the government arena. The following problems represent only a small subset for the introduction of intelligent software systems.

- Conversion
- Computer-aided instruction
- Signal processing, pattern recognition, and analysis
- Natural language understanding and processing
- Logistics support
- Command, control, and communication
- Intelligence analysis
- Battlefield management

Upon examination of specific problems in the above area, as well as in others, you will find a pressing need to use integrated artificial intelligence, cooperating expert systems, distributed artificial intelligence, domain-specific shell technology, and time-critical artificial intelligence methods. The problems associated with the government tend to be large and heavily constraint oriented with severe performance characteristics. They require the subtlest combination of traditional and heuristic technology.

Many of the applications in the process, manufacturing, and government systems have a real-time characteristic and require extensive reasoning and intelligent handling of combinatorially explosive problems in meaningful time frames. Addressing these problems with straightforward brute force usually leads to unsuccessful results. It is by the subtle application of knowledge, heuristics, intelligence, and reasoning combined with high-performance traditional methodologies, as is appropriate, that you can reduce the combinatorially large problem down to polynomial run time. This aspect is key when you are considering developing and delivering knowledge-based applications on systems such as the VAX. You must effectively reason to focus your attention and to reduce the inherent complex nature of the underlying problem itself.

Intelligent Conversion

An area that is worth some exploration is intelligent conversion. It is a problem that is of great importance to the government arena and industry at large. Although it is a problem that is characterized by a well-described input domain, as well as a well-described output domain, it can easily become combinatorally explosive and severely compute intensive if not done appropriately.

Since the 1950s, one of the most continual and persistant of all problems has been that of conversion. Time and time again, data processing departments, applications engineering groups, and every other functional group related to computing have encountered the unpleasant experience of having to convert something to something else. In some cases it might be from one operating system to another. More often than not it has taken the shape and form of converting from one programming language to another. Database conversions have become commonplace, as have operational methodologies. An audit of the dollars that are spent on an annual basis related to computing would reveal that an alarmingly large fraction has to do with conversions as opposed to the fundamental generation of new computing capability.

It is quite obvious that although this process has been going on for some 30 plus years, very little in the way of automation to make this process computerized and more efficient has taken place. Take for example the governments mandate with respect to Ada. There is now a requirement that all new systems be implemented around the Ada programming language. This becomes extremely difficult in light of the many, many computing applications and services that reside in a non-Ada implementation. The process of converting what exists to Ada is monumental.

A further example has to do with training. Today, there are computer-based instruction (CBI) systems or authoring systems. These systems allow for a simplistic form of training with course-based material. Presently, the methodology for making use of the CBI or authoring systems is massively manually intensive. Given that you already have a paper course, it usually requires hundreds of hours to convert that material into the framework of the authoring system. When you look at the backlog of source course material and make some rough calculations, the conversion into CBIs becomes prohibitive in time, as well as dollars, on almost any scale you choose.

Some of the most painful computer experiences can come from conversions. Frequently, technical staffs experience entropy, confusion, and frustrationas when they are confronted with taking something that works in one environment and getting it to reliably work in a consistent fashion in another environment. In the VAX world you can draw many similar analogies: converting a DBMS database application to a relational-oriented Rdb application or converting a user interface that currently runs under UIS to a user interface under another graphics paradigm. Moving a forms application under FMS to one that resides under TDMS is another example.

Artificial intelligence tools, concepts, and techniques hold great promise in the area of intelligent conversions. This area has not been exploited at all in an industrial fashion. Yet from a return on investment viewpoint, it holds great promise when compared with many other opportunities. There are three general classes of the intelligent conversion problem. The first is an expert system that would convert a manual operation into a computerized operation. The second is an expert system that would convert a partially computerized operation along with some aspects that are still manual into a computerized operation. The third is an expert system that would convert a computerized operation into another computerized operation. There are other possible classes of conversion, but the above three capture the spirit and the opportunities associated with the general problem.

Inherently, you are confronted with building a knowledge-base converter that can operate intelligently over an input domain to generate a consistent and verifiable point in a target conversion range. The knowledge base would contain both declarative and procedural representation and logic for the following key areas. The domain would have to be fully described. The domain characterizes the input or starting point of the conversion process. For instance, if you were converting from one programming language that was used to implement an application into another programming language, the domain in terms of the knowledge about the input language and the nature and characteristics of the input application would have to be fully described. Only by the knowledge-base converter having knowledge of both the source programming language and the source application could successful conversion ensue. Next, knowledge would have to be contained to totally describe the target range.

In the above example, the range would have one key component that is the knowledge describing the target language or output programming environment. The assumption here is that the application is being held fixed. If the application was also going to be mutated in some fashion, this knowledge would have to be described in the knowledge-base converter. The knowledge-base converter would need information on various goals associated with the conversion process. These goals might take the form of performance specifications, desires in terms of architecture, and structured implementation and specifications on how you derive functionality. It would be important to contain in the knowledge base a set of metrics that could be used to evaluate the quality of the conversion process. These metrics would be necessary in order to evaluate whether or not the goals of conversion are being met and indeed in what direction the knowledge base needs to reason to improve the quality of the conversion.

Finally, the knowledge base should contain a suite of information and logic that would allow it to do test and evaluation in an intelligent fashion so as to improve the result that is obtained automatically in the target range. The last and perhaps the most key component of the knowledge-base converter would be a knowledge algorithm that would allow this expert system to perform the intelligent conversion from the input point in the domain to a specified and constrained output point in the range. This knowledge algorithm would be highly problem

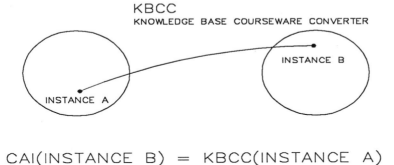

INPUT DOMAIN
PAPER—BASED COURSEWARE

OUTPUT RANGE
EXISTING AND FUTURE CAI'S AND ICAI'S

KBCC
KNOWLEDGE BASE COURSEWARE CONVERTER

INSTANCE A

INSTANCE B

CAI(INSTANCE B) = KBCC(INSTANCE A)

Figure 10-5 Intelligent conversion process.

dependent and would require intelligent mechanisms to allow incremental search and refinement to ensue based upon repeated test
and evaluation. This would allow you to assess the metrics to allow intelligent navigation in the range, resulting in a satisfactory state with
respect to the goals.

An example stems from the immense problem that the military
faces in converting paper-based training systems into computer-based
instruction systems. Presently in the military there is a compendium
of many, many paper-based courses that have a specific format, source
content, and set of educational goals. There exists today a number of
authoring systems that when used interactively can produce a computer-based instruction environment. The conversion process is exceedingly manually intensive, requiring a vast amount of time to convert even one structured paper-based course into an acceptable computer-based instruction environment. An example of an intelligent
converter in this vast area would be a knowledge-based courseware
converter (KBCC) for the military (see Figure 10-5). The domain in
this case is the particular class of paper-based courses that would be
the input to the conversion process. For a particular type of course,
there are standards that are associated with the format, sequence of
presentation of the information, examination of the student, and
presentation of the source material. The domain in the knowledge-
based courseware converter would have knowledge to understand this

highly structured and organized input and the general knowledge associated with the physics and architecture of the source input training material.

The range in this particular example constitutes a particular authoring system. Again, these authoring systems are highly structured in their mechanisms and procedures of use. The problem is to take the input courseware material as it now exists and to convert it into a runnable computer-based instruction system using one of the targeted authoring systems. Many goals would be associated with this process. Some of those goals stem from trying to mimic as closely as possible the structure, presentation, format, and usability of the paper course in a mirrored computer-based instruction environment. Other goals would stem from a strong desire to exploit some of the advantages of a CBI environment over inflexible and immutable paper. Metrics would have to be specified for the knowledge-based courseware converter to be able to intelligently navigate this problem. One metric would be associated with the completeness and consistency of the conversion. Another would be associated with adhering to the sequence and format of the specified course material under consideration. In this problem, it will be important to automate and computerize the capturing of the text associated with the input courseware material. Given the highly structured nature of the input material, a restricted domain language processor would suffice for doing text manipulation, mapping, and intelligent packaging once the characters were captured in a digital fashion. This facility would also be a part of the knowledge-base courseware converter (see Figure 10-6).

You might take the source material and scan it through an optical character reader and post that material into a digital database. Upon demand during its intelligent reasoning process, the knowledge-based courseware converter could access the raw digital form of the course, using the restricted domain language processor, to understand key words and phrases in the process of aligning the source material with the structure of the training content and target CBI. The test and evaluation could be partly performed automatically and partly through human interaction with the target-generated authoring system. The automatic components could check for completeness, consistency, and structure of the associated target CBI system that was generated in the range. It would be important to make sure that the knowledge algorithm used in the courseware converter could make use of the interactive criticism by a human evaluator in conjunction

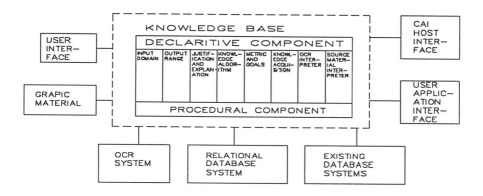

Figure 10-6 Knowledge-based courseware converter.

with the goals and metrics that are in the knowledge base to intelligently search the range to iteratively refine the target generated CBI.

Intelligent technology such as expert systems can dramatically improve the woeful state of affairs that exists with respect to conversions in the industrial and the government sector today. Knowledge-based technology that would capture the physics and specifications of the domain, as well as the range, using a flexible search-based knowledge algorithm to perform the conversion, based upon knowledge of goals, metrics, test, and evaluation would substantially improve the current process. The VAX is an ideal system on which to build such knowledge-based converters. Many of the opportunities that exist for conversion are already in the VAX environment. Where better to build and implement the knowledge-based converter than on the VAX. Indeed, you might have a conversion problem that is IBM based and still perform the knowledge-based conversion intelligently on the VAX. With its tremendous collection of sophisticated heuristic and traditional programming environments, it presents an ideal environment for such an expert system.

In-depth research will uncover much reusable technology in the area of intelligent conversions. The one aspect that will be highly class dependent, if not problem dependent in a given class, will be the knowledge conversion algorithm. But even this piece of technology should be fairly general and highly reusable across a large collection of instances in a particular class of conversion problems. Whether this area for expert systems is pursued internally by organizations to alleviate their own conversion burdens or attacked aggressively by vendors to offer flexible, generic solutions such as a conversion package to convert from Fortran to Ada, much progress will be made in the next few years in the VAX environment.

Other Vertical Markets

The process and general manufacturing industries and the government arena are only three tangible examples of vertical markets with broad and profound application opportunities for intelligent software. In general, all other the vertical markets follow these three in terms of the breadth and depth of opportunity. Other vertical markets that present great promise and in which development and delivery is already underway include:

* Medicine
* Management information systems and data processing
* Finance
* Insurance
* Graphic arts
* Law

The greatest opportunity for AI is approaching problems that are industry specific with a broad application. This is not to say that highly specific problems unique to a particular process, site, or company are not worth solving. But if AI and expert systems are to have the impact that other technologies have had, it is going to be by the building of intelligent vertical market applications that follow the format of domain-specific shells. This represents, by and large, the great challenge and the great opportunity for this new technology over the next years.

11

Additional Applications

Choosing an Appropriate Application

One of the fundamental problems that confronts all organizations is getting started in artificial intelligence and expert systems. Many times the technology itself is not nearly as elusive as an appropriate selection of a domain or a problem to attack. Again and again, organizations display uncertainty about just what are the central problems and applications to be approached. At one level the answer to this seems obvious, and many organizations have undertaken widely diverse intelligent applications development. At another level the question is quite complicated and has seriously impeded the progress of vendors and end-user organizations. Moreover, of the many projects that have been started, very few have actually produced truly tangible results. This is because there are basic issues and concepts that are not commonly recognized that pertain to the selection of an appropriate project or product in the area of expert systems.

The problem becomes clearer if we restate our central definition of AI: Artificial intelligence is a set of tools, concepts, and techniques which allows you to address problems that cannot be solved in a closed-form analytic solution. Again, what this definition tends to do is to demystify AI and remove a lot of the expectations associated with it — and therefore to make you more realistic about what AI can accomplish. AI and expert systems are just another approach to automating problems on a computer. If you see it as more than that you are likely to attack problems, projects, and products that are unrealistically difficult with today's technology and skill base.

The Steps in Choosing an Appropriate Application

The first step in choosing an appropriate problem is to forget about artificial intelligence and expert system technology altogether. If you start out with the attitude of a solution in search of a problem rather than a problem in search of a solution, you will probably end up frustrated and disappointed in your results. Most end users know where the opportunities are and usually those opportunities manifest themselves by having real ROI benefits to their solution and indeed produce automation. Fundamentally, any of these problems, if they're worth solving, have as the likely reason some meaningful AI content associated with the solution. Moreover, you should be careful in reviewing the class of all problems that present an opportunity. Progress stems from a firm underpinning and a tangible framework. Nothing could be further from the truth than the belief that an algorithm is not necessary to build an expert system. If there is no algorithm, there is no way other than random processes to accomplish the task at hand.

When you consider which problem, or project, or product to build, you should take the conservative view and choose those projects or problems that have the highest content of traditional mathematical systems analysis and systems engineering. A common misconception is that if operations research or another traditional discipline can prove effective, maybe it's really not worth applying AI techniques. Nothing could be further from the truth. It has been found over the years that the larger the problem, the greater is the necessity to have a solid mathematical structure and description for it at some level. A good problem — a good application — is one in which you can combine mathematical modeling and analysis with some heuristic reasoning to arrive at the solution.

The third issue in selecting a problem is to make sure that for the heuristic component, which cannot be described fully or adequately in utilizing traditional mathematical approaches alone, there is adequate domain knowledge present to solve the problem. A lot of people find this statement amusing, but it is very true. I am not one of those enthusiasts who loves the common practice of cloning old Elmer's mind. Unfortunately, when you only have old Elmer to work with many times you capture his bad reasoning processes along with his good reasoning processes. A good problem for intelligent automation is one in which you have ready access to a number of domain experts who can be involved on a routine basis to arrive at a realistic and robust heuristic component. This issue becomes critical if you are going to attempt to build a domain-dependent solution shell as opposed to a one-shot expert system or a simple replacement for an individual.

It is very important to state that a good problem is also characterized by a strong interest and great excitement on the part of management. Vision is necessary by these people. The solution of very few of these projects is quick and easy. Unless there are senior people who are committed to solving the problem, the expert system project will frustrate most of the management staff long before it has a chance to bear fruit.

Common-sense reasoning represents another discriminator in the selection of an appropriate problem. In the solution of any problem there is some aspect of common sense. Common-sense reasoning in an expert system can be modeled. However, it is very costly. In the paradigm of a production rule-based system it requires many rules to capture this surface and broad-based type of logic. In general, you should choose a problem that has as little common-sense reasoning and as much domain-specific physics associated with it as possible.

In the process of trying to decide what to work on it can be very illuminating to sit down with representative domain specialists from each of the problem areas. Ask them within a 2-hour period to jot down on a piece of paper the description of exactly how they go about solving their problem. Usually if it is difficult to extract that information and if there are a lot of unwritten rules, knowledge engineering difficulties probably will ensue. You are going to be confronted in any project with the knowledge engineering process of extracting the information. The domain experts who the project team will work with are a key component. All things being equal, if the domain experts in one area are articulate and capable of describing in some format (including pictures, schematics, narrative paragraphs, data sheets, case examples, or any other mechanism) how they work, you are going to make excellent progress. I have been confronted time and time again with inarticulate domain specialists. Even with the worst of them, you can eventually, through an iterative process of observation, question and answer, and the like to find out what's going on. Constructing a limited prototype and getting them involved in criticizing it when it makes a right decision or a wrong decision can greatly aid this process. However, if they don't freely divulge how they do what they do, they will become a key impediment to developing the intelligent application.

Another issue that should be actively dealt with in the selection of an appropriate application has to do with time criticalness and the overall systems requirements. Unless something is delivered into production that meets mainstream requirements, the project will eventually lose steam and the technology in the organization will be discredited. A clear understanding of integration requirements, distribution acquirements, delivery platforms, maintenance and modularity, verification and validation, performance, and throughput is absolutely essential up front in application evaluation. If an organization is not prepared to do integrated artificial intelligence and commit to large traditional systems and applications engineering along with the expert system components, these types of applications should be avoided.

There are many problems that can be solved in a very loosely coupled advisory mode. These problems have far less critical systems requirements. I have found, however, that in working with organizations from the process industries, the financial industries, general manufacturing, as well as graphic arts, that the big ROI problems manifest requirements of tight integration, distribution, and time criticalness. If you choose one of these problems, be very realistic about what you're getting into. Moreover, it becomes absolutely key that in the early stages of knowledge engineering and prototyping that you spend time in making those efforts in accordance with real delivery requirements. By and large, porting is an illusion. Most organizations actually end up in a substantial rewrite phase when the true systems and global environment issues are understood and finally addressed. If your organization is not prepared to make this type of commitment, don't choose such a problem. Experience has taught that in problems that require integration, distribution, time criticalness, and many other real-world mainstream features the VAX computing environment and its associated product line present by far the best technology and product foundation to build upon.

Another important aspect in problem selection is a clean understanding of what software tools are going to be used to solve the problem. Unfortunately, this is by and large given limited thought and insight. Not all problems require the same tools. Certain tools are more complicated and difficult to utilize than others. Certain problems require many more tools than others. In the process of selecting an appropriate problem, it is key to identify what is going to be needed in the way of computer environments. If you believe all that you need is one tool, you either have a very simple problem or you have a very limited exposure to solving things in the real world. If the latter is the case, you're going to set back expert systems and AI in your organization because time will be wasted complaining about how that tool or that vendor is not providing what is needed. Many tools will be needed to do the job and unless you're committed to building an organization and a design center philosophy to utilize those tools, you should choose a problem which is very limited in scope.

In most of the problems it becomes apparent that the amount and the complexity of traditional computer science involved in building and deploying a solution to a problem that has meaningful AI content is drastically underestimated. Be prepared that in a real-world problem of this type you will be spending as many dollars and have as many people worrying about traditional systems engineering, systems analysis, computer science and programming facilities as you will have knowledge engineers that are attempting to clone the mind of old Elmer.

When you inventory the potential problems that are worth attacking in an organization, you should be careful not to choose problems that require sophisticated learning facilities as well as justification and explanation facilities. In artificial intelligence and expert systems we have a technology that holds tremendous promise. For this technology there are many examples of toy systems that manifest interesting human-like characteristics. There are very few examples of deployed systems that live up to the expectation of the popularized literature and seminar circuit. My recommendation in general is not to attack AI problems that you don't already have a firm underpinning of science to address unless your organization will accept a very long and expensive development cycle. There have been projects that I have been associated with that have resulted in the development and codification of many new state-of-the-art techniques with respect to AI. But these projects have been long in their development cycles and very expensive.

Associated with every problem is the expectation of its solution and its worth. Problems should be attacked that have enough of an expectation and worth so that true interest is manifested by management, yet not so great that the whole philosophy and organizational structure being established may be jeopardized. Expectations are very subtle in AI. Almost from the outset the mere mention of AI and expert systems stirs unrealistic expectations. Be especially careful in the selection of a problem that could not have expectations managed during the life cycle of the project. The solution to the problem and indeed progress in general will be tough enough. Overselling what can be accomplished can become an unmanageable situation for the development team and indeed for the organization itself to live with. Get your feet wet and deliver something. Then get your feet wet again and deliver something again. When you have a track record of delivery, then contemplate attacking a problem for which the expectations associated with its solution, as well as its worth, are large.

With respect to expert systems that have meaningful AI components, choose an evolutionary approach, rather than a revolutionary approach, to problem selection. Addressing a problem that is already solved or solvable to a certain degree of satisfaction, where the addition of AI content would make the solution a little better, is a wonderful way to make tangible progress. Attacking a problem that has completely escaped automation or has frustrated the management staff by the absolutely unacceptable results of the present automation attempts sets up an environment that can potentially lead to catastrophic project failure. You should not feel less of an AI scientist and a knowledge engineer by building on top of a firm computerized foundation that already exists.

Unfortunately, given the current state of artificial intelligence and expert systems in the real world, learning is doing and doing is learning. By and large you will have very few if any case studies, previous designs, implementations, or other underpinnings to rely on. You are going to be confronted with a frustrating process at best. Remember this when you select your candidate applications. In an evolutionary sense, artificial intelligence technology and expert systems will have a major operational impact on the way the world markets, manufactures, makes decisions, and operates. However, if the rate of success is not improved through careful and appropriate problem selection, once again this discipline might be discredited. Artificial intelligence technology and expert systems is here today. Only a pragmatic, properly thought out set of approaches (see Figure 11-1) will keep artificial intelligence and expert systems technology evolving into that industrial reality that we all believe can happen.

○ Concentrate on the application, then on AI
○ Choose applications with a firm foundation
○ Make sure adequate domain knowledge exists
○ Choose an application that insures the interest of management
○ Stay away from applications that require common sense reasoning
○ Concentrate on problems in which the domain experts are cooperative
    and able to communicate their knowledge
○ Access system requirements carefully before you choose
    an application area
○ Choose problems with a meaningful ROI, avoid problem areas at first
    where expectations cannot be managed
○ Avoid problems at first where extensive coding might be necessary
○ Choose applications in conjunction with software tool understanding
○ Concentrate on applications with well-understood AI
    paradigm requirements
○ Choose an application that builds on top of existing solutions
○ Concentrate on applications where delivery is natural

Figure 11-1   Choosing an appropriate application.

Intelligent Computer-Aided Instruction

One of the most pervasive problems that all industries and governments face is that of training employees and citizens. The dollars expended in this nation on training people to perform tasks and functions is mind boggling on any scale. Intelligent computer-aided instruction holds vast potential to more efficiently fulfill the requirements that are desperately needed in today's industrial and commercial environments. All too often industry is faced with the problem of maintaining skill level in both its operational, manufacturing, and technical staffs. This problem is not an easy one as the complexities of design and manufacture increase. Additionally, the government in its military responsibilities, as well as its role in education, faces a monumental task in the training of individuals. A classic example in the military would be training people to maintain complicated weapon systems. The complexity of those systems and the skills required in maintaining them presents a formidable task. A characteristic example of training in the industrial sector stems from the process industries. There you are confronted with the need for skilled plant and process operators. As plant personnel retire, those skills are not easy to come by in any traditional fashion. The motivations and benefits for developing intelligent computer-aided instructional systems are strong and pervasive throughout every segment of our society.

For the last 15 years, the academic world has been active in studying how AI and knowledge-based techniques might lend themselves to producing high-quality, efficient, and truly intelligent training and tutoring environments. As yet, there have not been a great number of commercial successes. This is not to say that there are not training systems or computer-aided instruction systems or computer-based instruction systems available on the market. Computer-based instruction systems have been available for many years now. The systems that presently exist are very inflexible and unintelligent as to how training is actually conducted for a particular group or student. A knowledge-based approach would have a number of characteristics and goals that are not found presently in any training environment. One characteristic is to be able to develop hand-tailored curriculums instead of having a static notion of training needs. The fundamental training material and information should be organized in a very atomic fashion. You might envision having a database such as Digital's Rdb as the global knowledge base on which there are atoms of training which represent the smallest training entities that you might be concerned with. In addition, there would be molecules and compounds of training leading to particular lesson structures. Ideally, through the utilization of the environment, these atoms, molecules, and compounds should produce hand-tailored lesson environments. Being able to describe the curriculum in terms of entities and attributes and being able to flexibly combine them is a key component to building an intelligent computer-aided instruction system.

There are a few other characteristics that such an AI application should have. One is the ability to dynamically build up a model of the student. The students in using the training environment will be providing key information as to the nature and characteristics of their own abilities to learn, whether they are quick learners or slow learners, and what they retain and forget. Having a model that can learn about the student and develop his or her characteristics of learning intelligently is a necessary component to building an intelligent computer-aided instruction system.

It is important to have a way of reasoning about training strategy and from that strategy to be able to reason about a tactic of training considering a particular student. This strategy of training is based upon intimate knowledge of the student that would be garnered from the reasoning module that builds up the student model. Another important aspect of this instruction system is the student interface. It is important not only to present the curriculum in a fashion that is interesting and easy to learn, but it is necessary to get dynamic feedback from the student in order to learn how well that student is doing. This leads to a dynamically changing student module. There are many levels of complexity that such a student interface could be built around. These span from choosing multiple choice responses to filling in the blanks to selecting from a finite collection of responses to having a true natural language parser that understands free-form typed responses and questions from the student. In looking at the spectrum of possible student interfaces, you can see that this in itself can have a very large AI content. The most desirable student interface would be built around a combination of intelligently presented and reasoned forms that can be dynamically built and modified, as well as natural language understanding. The student interface would not only be essential in presenting a curriculum that would be dynamically generated from the knowledge base of entities and attributes of training, but would be key to garnering the information necessary for the student model to be able to reason.

A central aspect of an ICAI system is its tutoring component. This module is essentially a curriculum-independent module that would moderate lesson plans and formulate the nature of the presentation of course material. Basic to the tutor is its ability to figure out exactly what the student is learning and what the student is not. This has a high degree of AI content, as much as the module that dynamically builds up the student model. The tutor essentially is that reasoning component that figures out ideally how to get the student from here to there. It must take in what the student currently knows, where the student has been having great success, and where the student has been having great difficulties and formulate the insightful new lesson to make maximum training take place. If the tutor does its job and the dynamically built student model is correct, optimal high-quality training should ensue.

An additional component in building an intelligent computer-aided instruction system is the student dialogue manager. The student dialogue manager performs intelligent reasoning in diagnosing what the student knows at any point in time, as well as formulating the strategic and tactical responses back to the student to maximize the learning process. The diagnostic functioning of the student manager is particularly AI oriented. An issue such as the identification of buggy responses or a response that indicates misconception or error on the part of the student has a high degree of heuristic content if it is to be done appropriately. The ability to formulate strategic responses is an outgrowth of the ability of this module to understand the goals of the particular lesson as well as inputs from the student model and other strategies that are important. How you respond to the student in a dialogue fashion tactically can either greatly improve the quality of the training experience or limit it. Decisions such as whether or not the lesson should be continued become key. If you are losing the student, perhaps the best thing to do is to do something else. Sometimes, restating a particular question in another manner is appropriate. In any event, it becomes very important for the student dialogue manager to be able to intelligently interact with the tutor module so that the strategy of training can be dynamically changed to fit the present needs and requirements of the student.

A final module that is absolutely key is a global knowledge base. As indicated earlier, an ideal candidate would be Digital's relational datbase Rdb. It is a requirement for an intelligent computer-aided instruction system to have a stable storage architecture to be able to store not only the atoms, molecules, and compounds of training that are dynamically formulated but to have a repository of the state of training for any given student at any point in time.

An intelligent computer-aided instruction system can be viewed as a set of cooperating expert systems (see Figure 11-2). The cooperating expert systems include the student interface, the student modeler, the tutor, the curriculum repository, the student dialogue manager, and the global knowledge base. You can easily envision these modules being all contained in a single process or being entities that live in a design center of their own and that are distributable and relocatable over a network. In addition to cooperating expert system technology, intelligent computer-aided instruction cries out for a domain-specific solution shell approach.

It is obvious that atoms of curriculum content will change from application to application. Obviously, the curriculum associated with training on the maintenance of a military weapon system would be fundamentally different from those associated with training about a process in a batch-oriented pharmaceutical plant. However, everything else about the above-mentioned intelligent computer-aided instruction system is generic — it doesn't change. Intelligent computer-aided instruction is an ideal candidate for a domain-specific shell that

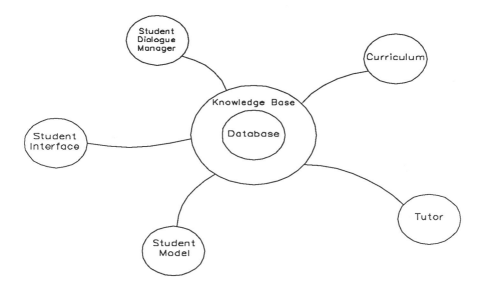

Figure 11-2   An architecture of an intelligent computer-aided instruction system.

is easily understood, without having to have any knowledge of computer science or artificial intelligence. This would be a shell in which the filling out of specific forms and the answering of certain questions would lead to a completed application to train anybody on anything.

It is obvious that integrated artificial intelligence will be a key component in devising such a shell. In an ICAI shell such as described above, many tools and facilities on the computer science level will have to be blended in an intelligent fashion to produce the high-quality result of intelligent computer-aided instruction.

There is another desirable aspect to vendors as well as end users in spending development dollars, as well as other resources, in developing intelligent computer-aided instruction systems. With other expert and knowledge-based systems that are going to have a more direct effect on the live operations of an organization, there are many concerns. For instance, if you are going to build an intelligent control system to introduce into the feedback loop of a particular plant, immediately the question is asked, What happens if that knowledge base makes a mistake? What is it going to do to the process? What is it going to do to the manufacturing line? There are questions of verification and validation of the knowledge base, time-critical responsiveness, as well as simple fears and phobias on the part of operational, as well as managerial personnel in the deployment of such a new state of the art technology. However, few organizations or individuals feel threatened by the thought of bringing in an intelligent computer-aided instruction system. The issues of putting the organization out of business if this technology stumbles are totally disarmed by the nature of what the system is intended to do. There is not a single industry or sector of government that could not benefit dramatically by having artificial intelligence, expert system, and knowledge-based technology applied intelligently to the area of computer-aided instruction. The solution to this problem will require an intelligent use of integrated artificial intelligence, cooperating expert systems, distributed artificial intelligence, and domain-dependent solution shell technology. It is time that the tremendous body of material from the academic environment is converted into standard off-the-shelf product capability. In the upcoming years, this area will make a lot of commercial progress industrially. The motivation is strong, the market demand is high, and the VAX computational environment is absolutely ideal for this application of AI technology.

Intelligent Databases

One of the hot areas of research, development, prototyping, and application is to take the world of artificial intelligence and marry it to traditional databases. This marriage of technology (see Figure 11-3) is important not only to solving problems in the traditional MIS DP area, but to producing high-quality expert system applications that have firm MIS and database technology underpinnings.

These two information-based opportunities for the introduction of artificial intelligence represents most of the activity in this field that is taking place in the United States today. The first, the merging of AI technology into mainstream MIS DP environments stems from the desire to streamline and simplify many of the operational problems associated with designing, maintaining, and using large database systems in Fortune 1000 computing environments. Many problems in this area have gone wanting for solutions for a very long time. The second area of marrying these two technologies stems from the architectural and design limitations of most of the expert system shells

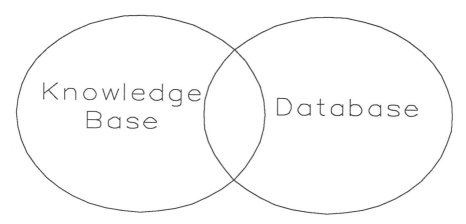

Figure 11-3 A marrying of two technologies.

that exist in the world today. By intelligently marrying a database such as Digital's Rdb to a shell you can overcome many of the limitations that the shell has when addressing real-world applications.

Relational databases provide a natural target for this type of marriage. The relational model forms a very well-defined closed algebra. Likewise, the AI paradigms of reasoning and, in particular, declarative representation also form a closed algebra. It is because of this that you can very intelligently merge AI tools, concepts, and techniques in a paradigmatic fashion, as well as a data fashion, to relational databases. Exploiting this provides you with the architectural foundation for building intelligent databases and intelligent database-driven applications.

Query optimization represents an important potential application of this type. SQL is becoming a standard among database vendors in terms of how people interact with the underlying relational database. Writing efficient SQL queries that do not require vast amounts of CPU time to execute is not a trivial task. More often than not this requires a very senior and talented person who spends a lot of time at a terminal tying up many mainframes. An expert system that would allow you to interactively design and test SQL queries against the real database would be valuable. In large database environments it becomes very important to be able to develop new query-based applications in an efficient manner. An expert system such as this would justify itself relatively easily.

Another area of great concern in marrying AI into traditional MIS DP operations is that of database design. Presently, it takes very senior people to design and adjust new databases. An expert system that would alleviate this burden and dramatically simplify the problem would be highly desirable. This database design capability should be intelligently coupled with performance management and data management capabilities. The expert system should minimize the difficulties of developing on an initial database; in addition, it should monitor the utilization of that database and recommend modifications and restructuring based upon the use of and the performance in a particular application. Today, data management and performance management of large databases is a highly time-consuming task in most organizations. If the data environment gets large enough, it usually requires armies of people to maintain some level of control. An expert system such as the one described above would dramatically alleviate some of the costs and frustrations associated with this process in MIS DP environments.

The world is comprised of many databases. Over the last few years the trend has been strongly to the relational model. Many organizations are confronted with having lots of databases under older hierarchical, network-like structures and a strong desire to bring those databases into the relational world. The conversion problems can be very severe. An expert system that could look over an existing database and map it into the relational model and then go ahead and convert the existing databases would reduce both the time and the effort for many MIS DP organizations. The main problem in this area is not one of converting the data, but of converting the representation and the model. This mapping problem of one database model into another is an ideal candidate for an expert approach and one that almost every major corporation could benefit from. Once a database application is deployed, the utilization of it becomes an additional opportunity for AI. The spirit of relational databases is one of interactive, online, *ad hoc* queries. In this arena, natural language processing front ends hold a vast potential. Much work has been done by many vendors to provide intelligent front ends to databases that would allow operational people in an MIS DP applications environment to query and update the database grammars. To the extent that this can be done, you can dramatically reduce the costs and enhance the usability of most database applications.

In contrast to the above, a further motivation for the marrying of AI and databases stems from the building and addressing of intelligent expert system applications. Databases provide many facilities, including that of a stable storage structure that does not reside in the virtual address space of a computer. Very advanced reporting facilities, journaling and logging facilities, security systems, and the like are routine components of database systems. By joining heuristic environments to traditional databases such as Digital's Rdb, you can inherit the characteristics of Rdb in an expert system application. To build an intelligent order entry system or an intelligent scheduling system, you should have a solid database MIS foundation at the very kernel of the application. Surrounding this kernel should be a number of intelligent inference-based modules that could tightly and efficiently interact with the relational database to provide the overall applications and systems functionality. This architectural insight is key to building extensible expert systems that have industrial strength characteristics. It has been found over the years that marrying a relational database such as Digital's Rdb with AI tools, concepts, and techniques right away in the architecture, design, and implementation of an application, has led to much higher-quality expert system results. A further merging of these two technologies stems from the desire to build intelligent databases. There are two approaches to this. One approach starts out from scratch and reduplicates all of the services that traditional databases offer and adds the new concepts of inferencing. This is opposed to the more practical approach of starting out with a fine traditional database and extending its functionality to include intelligent inferencing. My present point of view and my work have centered around the latter approach.

Many people in the real world would like to build a database application in which the database in some sense itself could extract patterns and inferences from the underlying data that is being stored away. This pattern extraction can be accomplished very naturally by tightly coupling any of the state-of-the-art expert system shells in a compiled fashion with any of the relational databases. The pattern extraction and inferencing can be made to look transparent to the user of the application. An exact definition of an intelligent database does not exist. However, by taking a database such as Digital's Rdb and tightly marrying it with heuristic programming environments and expert shells, you can produce an environment in which most of the relevant real-world needs could be naturally addressed. The modern relational databases provide for the abilities to reason about their representation, as well as to incrementally refine their structure on the fly. The hooks to having self-modifying, self-describing, and self-regulating intelligent databases that seem to do automatic inferencing both on incoming and outgoing control structures is possible with a coordinated approach given today's technologies.

Many developers are using object-oriented programming environments and techniques to construct their applications. It would be of great benefit to have a fully functional object-oriented database so that any time a construct in the object-oriented environment gets created or manipulated a similar structure is created or manipulated in the underlying object-oriented database. This could be pragmatically accomplished by building this capability on top of a high-quality relational database. You would have the capability of a stable storage environment for inheritance taxonomies, methods, and messages in addition to what the traditional object-oriented environments give you by way of the virtual address space. Creating an object-oriented database transparently out of a relational database and marrying it to an object-oriented paradigm such as flavors is practical with today's technologies.

Taken to its logical conclusion, the marriage of artificial intelligence with relational databases provides an ideal foundation for generating an extraordinarily intelligent and high-quality application generation environment. For many years, companies have been vending fourth-generation language approaches and simple database application generators in the industrial world. Some of these have been highly successful in a commercial sense. The ability to build a true and easy to use database application generation environment in which programming tasks, as well as computer science is kept to an absolute minimum, and in which the underlying system takes care of all the intimate details, relies very heavily on building this capability on top of an intelligent marriage of AI and database.

The motivations for joining these two technologies are very strong (see Figure 11-4). The concepts and tools to work with are now stable enough to allow meaningful progress with an acceptable risk. No doubt sometime in the future there will be new products that are not the result of marrying existing products but that are fundamentally a design merging of these two technologies. To date, no products exist in the world with this characteristic. The expert system shells fall dramatically short in the areas in which traditional databases shine, and the traditional databases look extraordinarily primitive in their modeling and reasoning capability when compared to what can be done with a high-quality shell. Eventually, industry will respond to this opportunity with a generation of products that presents the best o Query optimization

o Database conversion

o Database performance management

o Natural language front end

o Automatic database inference

o Object-oriented databases

o Application generation

o Multiuser distributed synchronization

o Stable storage for expert systems

Figure 11-4 Intelligent database opportunities.

of both. Today, there is the opportunity to intelligently marry what exists to produce this highly desirable environment to address many industrial problems.

Intelligent Computer-Aided Software Engineering (ICASE)

The Motivation for ICASE

Software development is currently a very labor-intensive and skill-intensive endeavor for most organizations. All too often, a minimum amount of existing code is intelligently utilized in implementing a new application at a given organization when a new project is in development. It requires great knowledge on the part of software and systems developers to understand which existing code fragments should be utilized and how to best integrate them into the overall structure of the new application. Usually, this results in a minimum of leverage and a maximum time to develop the new application.

An ICASE environment would understand a particular domain such as scientific computation or process control. It would contain in its knowledge base information about existing code fragments as they relate to solving problems and building new applications in the domain. The ICASE environment would actively support the software engineering task when utilized by a developer attempting to implement

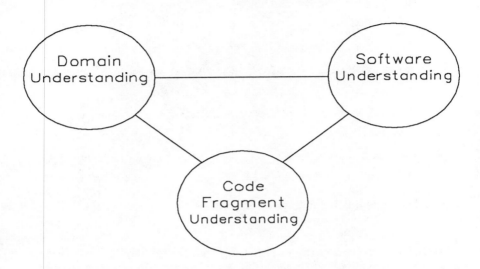

Figure 11-5   Key components of an intelligent computer-aided software environment.

a new application in the targeted domain based on existing and new capability (see Figure 11-5).

In most organizations there is extensive confusion and a high degree of entropy when new projects are begun. Intelligent support tools are necessary to streamline the architecture, design, and implementation process based upon corporate knowledge that exists or work that has already taken place. There are a number of traditional CASE tools that provide some aid in this area. Examples are Digital's code management system (CMS) and module management system (MMS). These systems allow you to organize existing code fragments, to be able to control their enhancements and modifications over time, and to be able to define an overall application in terms of the fundamental fragments.

However, they do not help you to understand how to use what exists or to understand what actually exists. Building a new application still requires extensive familiarity with the code fragments that are archived in the CMS libraries. Identifying and integrating these existing fragments in a new application is still difficult.

In the VAX computational environment, you can view an ICASE system as being layered around and tightly integrated with such existing CASE tools as Digital's CMS and MMS, resulting in an intelligent architecture, design, and implementation aid as opposed to a rather passive code management aid.

Benefits of ICASE

By subtly combining artificial intelligence and expert system technology with the concepts of CASE, you can produce an intelligent computer-aided software engineering environment that can actively aid in the architecture, design, and implementation of new applications. This ICASE environment should have an understanding of a particular application domain. For example, it could have the knowledge of a control engineer in building control systems. In addition, it would understand programming environments, as well as particular code fragments at the software engineering level. By subtly combining knowledge in a domain, along with understanding of software in general and the understanding of specific code fragments, a number of strategic and tactical benefits would result.

The first benefit would be to maximize the leverage of existing code at an organization. In most organizations people do not know where things exist, how to use them, and when to use them. All too often this results in rediscovering the wheel. A second benefit would be the subsequent minimization of the time to development. By having an active software engineering environment that made the architecture, design, and implementation process easier, that clearly presented those existing code fragments, and that could be utilized for a given application intelligently, great reductions in time and effort could be obtained.

A fundamental problem in most organizations is that of personnel turnover. All too often, there are only one or two people who really understand a particular code fragment or even a system. When these people leave the organization, more often than not their work becomes unsupportable or at least non-reusable. An ICASE environment would eliminate this undesirable effect of personnel turnover.

Overall, industry suffers from poor documentation and information transfer on the part of present software developers with respect to existing software capability. This results in a general software technology brittleness at most organizations. The ICASE environment would greatly minimize the costs associated with technology transfer and would make the overall organization robust in the face of new project demands in general.

Features and Functionality of an ICASE Environment

An ICASE system should provide a number of state-of-the-art features and functions to aid in the architecture, design, and implementation process of new applications. First, the ICASE environment should be a domain-specific shell that could utilize existing and future product capabilities in traditional CASE such as Digital's CMS and MMS layered software packages. By building the ICASE environment as a domain specific shell, you will make the process of teaching that environment about new code fragments and application domains straightforward. The goal of ICASE is not only to maximize the reusability of software technology and in-house technical knowledge but to make the ICASE environment itself reusable technology.

The ICASE environment will have an understanding of code fragments. This would include their input and output structure, as well as the features and functionality that a particular code fragment provides. Other characteristics of understanding would include performance, integration, and precision. Fundamentally, unless the ICASE environment can understand a particular code fragment or at least have limited knowledge of the design and implementation specifics of a particular code fragment, you cannot hope to build an environment such as the one we are describing.

In addition to the ICASE environment understanding individual code fragments, it would need to understand particular application domains. An example domain would be that of control engineering. If the ICASE environment did not have knowledge about control engineering, it could not actively aid in the architecture and design phases of new applications that are controls related. This, however, would not impede it from intelligently supporting the implementation phase in a decoupled sense.

By having knowledge of a particular domain, the ICASE environment could enter conceptual discourses at a higher level with a software developer and allow that software developer to rapidly prototype the architecture and design, as well as the implementation. Many domains would need to be supported. Such domains encompass finance, MIS, scientific computation, process control, and the like.

The ICASE environment would allow for straightforward knowledge acquisition techniques to teach it about new application domains, as well as new code fragments in any particular domain. Knowledge about code, as well as applications, would be added incrementally over time by the filling out of simple forms answering knowledge-base prompted questions and the drawing of schematic diagrams.

An important function of the ICASE system would be to contain knowledge of how to map characteristics, specifications, and functionality of a proposed new application onto the general problem domain, as well as existing code fragments in the knowledge base. It is this functionality that will allow the ICASE environment to actively aid in the architecture and design phases of a new project.

It would be important for the ICASE environment to have a highly graphically oriented user interface to aid the software developer in utilizing the system. This interface would be important not only in the active architecture, design, and implementation phases but in teaching the ICASE environment about new application domains, as well as code fragments in a given domain.

Ideally, the ICASE environment should have the ability to automatically understand and interpret code fragments from source file listings. This ability will be difficult to develop. However, artificial intelligence and expert systems do provide some answers and methodologies in this highly desirable area. It is not necessary to have automatic code understanding to build a highly beneficial ICASE environment. It is merely very desirable. First-generation ICASE environments will probably not have this capability and will require code understanding, meaning, and interpretation to be imparted by the software developer through the knowledge acquisition interface to the domain-specific shell. However, as this technology matures, it is highly likely that such a capability could be present in second- and third- generation ICASE systems.

Technical Direction for an ICASE Environment

Intelligent computer-aided software engineering represents a vast opportunity to make the software developer more productive in all phases of architecture, design, and implementation of new applications. An ICASE system would support the developer by actively being able to intelligently select those existing code fragments that could best be utilized in developing the new application. Further, it would be able to propose an initial architecture and design based on its domain knowledge from only a loose specification and dialogue with the end user.

The software developers would enter into a dialogue with the ICASE environment describing the characteristics, features, and functionality of the proposed new application. With this knowledge the ICASE environment would then analyze existing capability along with potential solution approaches to building the new application. The ICASE environment would graphically report back to the software developers a potential high-level architecture and design for the proposed application along with those code fragments that presently exist and can be meaningfully utilized. The existing code fragments would be present schematically in terms of the functionality that they would provide in the new application and graphics would indicate where in the high-level architecture and design these code fragments would be utilized.

This software engineering process between the human software developer and the ICASE environment would be iterative and incrementally refining. This would allow a natural convergence to the desired architecture, design, and implementation.

The process control industries offer an example. An ICASE environment for control engineers would contain knowledge about control theory and process engineering, as well as existing code fragments to implement control laws. In utilizing this environment, a software developer would enter into a dialogue describing the control requirements. This dialogue would capture the number of inputs and outputs to the control structure, as well as the desired control technology and control topology. In addition, the software developer would describe the relevant process elements and their characteristics that would be activated by the new control system. Specifications of the effectiveness of control such as gain margins, phase margins, transient, and steady-state response dynamics would be imparted by the software developer.

All of this information represents input to the ICASE environment (see Figure 11-6) for the particular new application to be developed. The ICASE environment would then apply its knowledge of control system design and architecture along with reasoning about the existing code fragments that have already been implemented. The ICASE environment would be essentially solving a computer-aided design problem, as well as a code understanding and reusability problem. The ICASE environment would subsequently report back to the control engineer or software developer an architecture, design, and an implementation. More often than not all the code that will be necessary to implement a new application will not exist. In this case, the

```
Type of Control System  _____

Process Technology  _____

Control Topology  _____

Process Topology  _____

Goal of Control  _____

Type of Disturbance  _____

Nature of Deadtime  _____

Precision  _____

Time Constant  _____

Scan Rate  _____

Stability Metric  _____

Tuning Metric  _____

              Control System Form
```

Figure 11-6   An example form for the ICASE of a new control system.

ICASE system will clearly indicate where new code needs to be written, and graphically indicate where existing code could be utilized.

It is highly likely that there would be more than one way to develop the new application. In this case, the ICASE system would present the multiple alternatives, allowing the software developer to pick, choose, and explore among them. In all likelihood the ICASE environment will have to query the software developer or control engineer to be more specific, to allow it to perform its tasks. In the above example, the ICASE environment might query the software developer as to whether or not deadtime compensation is important and whether the control structure should be designed for load disturbances, set point disturbances, or stochastic noise. It is by this highly interactive, high-level give and take dialogue that fast convergence on a desired architecture, design, and implementation could be arrived at.

The declarative component of the knowledge base for the ICASE environment will need to support structural and design taxonomies representing the application domain involved. In addition, it will need taxonomies that will contain the knowledge associated with any existing code fragments, as well as software in general. In the procedural component of the knowledge base, it will be necessary to model the methods, rules, and procedures associated with taking an application specification and solving the associated design problem.

The VAX computing environment provides an ideal foundation to build intelligent computer-aided software engineering environments on. There exist today many traditional CASE environments. A knowledge base that would be tightly integrated with these existing capabilities would provide a clear evolutionary path to a truly intelligent CASE environment. Only by developing ICASE tools can the tremendous costs and inefficiencies associated with software development be alleviated in the foreseeable future. Digital's code management system and module management system would provide an ideal starting point to develop an intelligent CASE environment. By utilizing the concepts of integrated artificial intelligence and domain-dependent solution shells, this capability could be efficiently and naturally developed.

Intelligent Graphic Arts

Motivation

The graphic arts industries are comprised of a number of segments such as newspaper, magazine, book, catalog, and the like. They are ideal candidates for the introduction of artificial intelligence and expert-system-based technology. This is because of the highly aesthetic nature of the fundamental design and production process. In particular, newspapers represent a supremely challenging and relevant environment for the introduction of this technology.

There are roughly 1700 newspapers in the United States today. All face the common problems of intelligently reserving space for a given edition, designing a particular paper, and then producing it. There exists extensive automation technology to aid this process. Sophisticated front-end editorial and classified systems alleviate the burden of text makeup. Moreover, there exist state-of-the-art graphic subsystems to allow the design and the development of art work and ads. What is lacking is an overall command, control, design, and production system to be able to tie the newspaper together in an intelligent electronic fashion.

Newspapers are comprised of many departments that presently work fairly autonomously. Most newspapers are under extremely tough deadline pressures and are under stress in producing a high-quality edition. Moreover, newspapers simultaneously work on multiple editions at the same time. All too often at a newspaper, conflicts arise between editorial requirements, advertising requirements, color requirements, press capacity, and general stylistic notions. These conflicts more often than not surface close to deadline and throw the staff of the newspaper into a veritable frenzy of activity. A set of cooperating expert systems that could intelligently automate the decision-making functions of a system, as well as a departmental viewpoint in an integrated fashion, would greatly benefit the industry.

You can presently view a modern day newspaper as comprised of a number of islands of automation. These islands do not talk with each other, nor is there a centralized decision making function which can arbitrate conflicts as early as possible instead of as late as possible. An example of a conflict would be a late-breaking ad by a major advertiser. It is difficult today for a newspaper to redesign an edition in a timely fashion, maintaining all of the rules of style to satisfy all department heads. A conflict like this arises many times a day at a major metropolitan daily. There are frequently heated debates between the advertising department, the editorial department, and the production department at or past deadline. These conflicts are always resolved but more often than not suboptimally. The results are usually economic inefficiencies at the newspaper.

At one level, all newspapers are created unequal. However, upon close inspection, there are strong central tendencies and common denominators to the functionality and decision-making process across most newspapers. The newspaper industry is an ideal candidate for the development of domain-specific solution shells to address the intelligent automation of the various design and decision-making functions. This would allow a given newspaper to easily configure the application for its site-specific rules, objectives, styles, data structures, prices, deadlines, and the like.

Benefits

There are many benefits to be had from the intelligent introduction of artificial intelligence and expert systems into the newspaper industry.

If you were able to design the paper more intelligently and resolve the conflicts early and optimally, subsequent savings in newsprint utilization and costs would follow. Presently, the decision-making and design functions are manual. This imposes later-breaking problems in the overall production process. To compensate for this, newspapers set their deadlines early to allow for the fact that extreme crisis management measures are going to be necessary and will take time to resolve. Intelligent automation would allow the newspapers to have later deadlines with the resulting increase in revenues, timeliness of news, and quality of the overall product.

Color is not a trivial problem to most newspapers. It puts demands on the space reservation function, the design function, and the production function. Dealing with color in a more intelligent and automated fashion would greatly increase the aesthetic and the ad revenue benefit components to the publication. Newspapers presently suffer from a phenomenon called credits and make goods. This stems from an ad that should have run in an edition having not run or an ad running that should not have. Moreover, out of place material because of the complexities of paper layout and design will again foster a credit or a make good to an advertiser. In addition to this cost, there is the lost revenue associated with suboptimal design of the newspaper as it relates to customer service.

Newspapers are under pressure to make their operations as efficient as possible given the economics of the industry. However, there is strong motivation to develop more zoned editions, as well as other feature and special-purpose products. Each one of these entities puts an increased burden on the entire infrastructure at a given publication. Intelligently automating the overall process would make it easy to design new products and experiment with them, as well as bring them online in a production sense, while minimizing the cost impact on the publication.

For the last 15 years the newspaper industry has been abuzz with the term pagination. Pagination refers to the full electronic automation of a newspaper, especially the ability to do full-page makeup electronically of any given page, including all text and artwork. A necessary component of pagination would be the intelligent automation of the other decision-making functions. It becomes obvious that unless you know at any point in time exactly what should go on a page, the benefits associated with full-page makeup cannot be entirely realized.

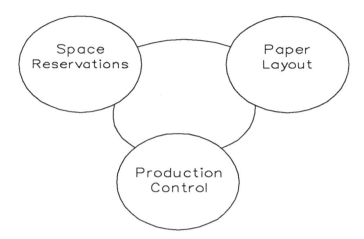

Figure 11-7   Functionality for an intelligent newspaper decision system.

The benefits of an intelligent automation system would be enormous to the average medium-to-large-scale newspaper. In the past, there have been attempts at such functionality using purely traditional approaches. These attempts have been made by vendors to the industry, as well as some large newspapers themselves. Overall, these attempts have fallen far short of the goals. This is because of the very large AI content involved in solving this automation problem.

The Systems

If you view a modern day newspaper from a systems viewpoint, you can break down the paper into three primary functions. These are space reservations, paper layout, and production control (see Figure 11-7).

The space reservation function is geared toward servicing the space requirements from both advertising and editorial points of view for any given edition as a front-end component to the overall process. You might view a newspaper as an entity in which all departments via for space in a given edition. These departments include editorial, classified advertising, and retail display advertising. The newspaper is a live entity in which there is a collection of editions that are constantly being worked on. Repeatedly through the life cycle of an edition the editorial, classified, and retail display departments are making dynamic and changing space requirements. Moreover, many of these requirements are serviced in an online fashion to advertising customers. The space reservation system must be able to intelligently take an order, price it, configure it at the high level, and provide adequate service to all departments concerned. In many ways, this function is characterized by a very intelligent database application.

Paper layout represents the heart of the newspaper environment. In this functional area, the newspaper is actually designed. There are three major aspects to this decision-making function. The first is the booking function in which the rough size of the edition is formulated, as well as the high-level layout. It is here that decisions are made as to the ordering of sections, section breaks, and the like. The next function is routinely referred to in the industry as the dummying capability. The dummy is the detailed low-level design of the newspaper, accounting for the placement of all editorial and advertising structures. It is here that such conflicts as the reluctance to position Ann Landers next to Erma Bombeck must be resolved. It is an exceedingly aesthetic and stylistic task rife with heuristics. The third major function of the paper layout area is press configuration.

You might view the final output of any pagination system as the printing press. A newspaper can only print what the printing presses allow. They are the ultimate determining factor to both the size of the paper, as well as the color content and overall aesthetic graphic look. Printing presses, by and large, represent a black art at a newspaper. There are usually one, two, or three individuals at most who really understand their operation and can configure the printing press to produce a given newspaper once the full dummy is generated for an edition. This area is also rife with AI content because of its highly object-oriented nature in representing its functionality.

The last major system in intelligently automating a newspaper would be production control. It is in this system that you must address the functionalities of the master scheduler. Scheduling and coordinating activities at a newspaper are highly complex. They are presently done on the fly, manually, and by the seat of the pants. It would be very important to have a system that could adjust deadlines to schedules and schedules to deadlines in an optimal fashion.

In addition to scheduling, the production control system would need to provide a material tracking and reporting function. This would be necessary so that the overall intelligent decision-making environment would know the status at any point in time of any piece of material.

All too often, an ad that is supposed to come in to the paper at one size actually arrives at the newspaper at a substantially different size. The production control system is the area in which staff, resources, materials, and distribution would be analyzed and factored into the overall automation structure at a given publication.

If done correctly, these three systems would provide a symphony of decision making capability at a newspaper. They would provide the much needed functionality to move the modern newspaper into the age of integrated decision making. Moreover, these systems would magnify the benefits associated with the technology that newspapers have already successfully applied.

Technical Direction

Space reservations, paper layout, and production control represent logical knowledge-based areas. Upon close examination, it will become obvious that each of these is actually a collection of expert systems themselves. All together, the entire environment is an ideal application for cooperating expert system technology. It would be very important to design these systems so that any system could stand on its own right. Newspapers, like most mainline industries, are not going to fully automate in any one step. A phased implementation approach is an absolute requirement.

However, upon the close examination of the physics of the underlying decision-making problem, it becomes apparent that these cooperating expert systems are strongly coupled. As deadline approaches, the space reservation system needs the feedback from the paper layout system to be able to decide whether or not a new request for space should be granted. The paper layout system receives its input from the space reservation system. The production control system decisions are highly dependent on a design of the newspaper. If the paper layout system alters that design in any manner at all, there will be an impact on the schedule and on the tasks necessary to produce the editions.

Conflict resolution between the peer cooperating agents will be absolutely necessary. In many ways, this conflict resolution mimics the process that takes place at a newspaper today. However, it would occur at electronic speeds and very early in the process instead of late in the process. Today, because of the highly autonomous nature of the various departments at a newspaper, conflicts are not even known

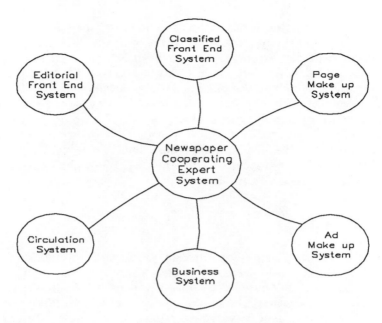

Figure 11-8   A cooperating expert system environment for the newspaper industry.

until close to deadline. Because of the totally integrated nature of the cooperating expert systems, these conflicts would be known when they happen, not when they were finally observed.

Integrated artificial intelligence will be very important in building such a system. Space reservations, paper layout, and production control have many traditional aspects along with their heuristic content. Database operations, as well as numerically oriented calculations, will be common place. Moreover, the intelligent environment will need to be tightly integrated into the other existing automation systems such as the traditional editorial and classified front-end systems (see Figure 11-8). The newspaper is presently a distributed environment. Moreover, newspapers have a high availability requirement. It is unacceptable that if a computer crashes or a disk fails the paper does not get printed on time. It will be necessary to utilize a multiple-CPU approach with backup to fulfill the operational requirements at a newspaper.

The problem of providing an intelligent space reservation, paper layout, and production control system to a major metropolitan daily is large and will be exceedingly computer intensive. Moreover, newspapers work on multiple editions at the same time in a highly dynamic environment, with tough deadline pressures. Time-critical artificial intelligence will be absolutely essential to the successful introduction of the technology to this application area.

The whole environment must be capable of supporting multiple modes of operation. These include automatic, interactive, manual override, and shadowed what if. In the automatic mode, the various cooperating expert systems perform their functionality in an autonomous fashion. At any point in time, personnel at the newspaper would interact with the experts through highly graphically oriented user interfaces. They might ask to see the layout of the paper, the configuration of the printing press, the space requirements, or the schedules. If they like what they see, they would simply leave the decisions and designs alone. If they didn't, they would ask for an explanation. If that explanation was unsatisfactory, in the interactive mode, they would suggest a new tactic, such as to make the paper larger or make the paper smaller but would leave the actual work to the cooperating expert systems.

In the manual override mode a member of the newspaper staff could specifically make a decision overriding anything that the expert systems decided. An example would be to move an ad from one location on one page to a new location on another page. In addition to the above modes of operation, it would be necessary to support a shadow what if mode that would allow the personnel at the newspaper to experiment with the edition and contrast it against the current excepted scenario. Presently, there are no mechanisms for exploring alternatives in the life cycle of an edition except those that are minor variations of the currently accepted central theme. The shadow what if capability would provide a vast decision-support aid in the life cycle of an edition.

The successful introduction of intelligent technology into a newspaper, on a broad scale, will require the application of the tools, concepts, and methodologies associated with integrated artificial intelligence, cooperating expert systems, distributed artificial intelligence, domain dependent solution shell, and time-critical AI. Without these technologies, the resultant application will be unsatisfactory with respect to the requirements of newspapers as they exist today and for the foreseeable future.

12

Conclusion

In this book we have covered the tools, techniques, and methodologies associated with:

* Integrated artificial intelligence
* Cooperating expert systems
* Distributed artificial intelligence
* Domain-dependent solution shells
* Time-critical AI

We have covered new methodologies of knowledge engineering and project organization that are more in line with the realities associated with addressing medium-to-large-scale knowledge-based applications. We have surveyed the various dimensions associated with tool selection and have clearly indicated the need and the opportunity to use a multitool approach to address problems on the VAX. We have delved into other issues, including development and delivery environments, knowledge representation, learning, justification and explanation, high availability, and verification and validation. Moreover, we presented a number of vertical market application areas spanning the process and general manufacturing industries, as well as the government arenas.

Intelligent technology is as much a reality as it is a goal, a state of mind. In particular, the intelligent use of the VAX on which to build intelligent applications on top of represents an important architectural, design, and implementation consideration and opportunity.

It is only by scientific well-thought-out and highly structured approaches combining the best of the world of traditional methods with those of heuristic methods that high-quality, flexible, and fully functional intelligent applications can be developed and delivered on the VAX.

The opportunities and application areas are varied. The challenge is to apply many technologies interwoven in a synergistic and mixed computing initiative fashion to uniquely address the need for intelligent applications on traditional architectures such as the VAX. Moreover, never lose sight of the fact that the VAX is not a LISP, C, or OPS5 machine, but rather is a solutions machine.

An industrial-strength cybernetic world is around the corner and intelligent applications residing on traditional hardware platforms will be the bridge leading to the new computing and industrial reality.

Appendix

Common Expert System Shells

The expert system shell environments which are listed are available on a broad range of traditional computer platforms, PCs, and special purpose computing environments.

AION CORP.
(415) 328–9595

Aion Development System
The Aion Development System is implemented using Pascal, some C and assembler. It uses rule-based, object-definition structures for its knowledge representation.

Aion Execution System
The Aion Execution System is implemented using Pascal, some C and assembler. It uses rule-based, object-definition structures for its knowledge representation.

ARITY CORP.
(800) PC–ARITY

Arity/Expert
The Arity/Expert Product is implemented using Prolog. It uses frame-based methods for its knowledge representation. This product sells for $295.

ARTIFICIAL INTELLIGENCE TECHNOLOGIES, INC.
(914) 347–6860

Mercury
The Mercury product is implemented using Common LISP. It uses schemas, frames, fact patterns, objects, networks, rules, scripts, methods, procedures and demons for its knowledge representation.

AUTOMATED REASONING CORP.
(212) 206–6331

Micro Intelligent Automatic Testing Equipment
The Micro Intelligent Automatic Testing Equipment product is implemented using C. It uses rule-based methods for its knowledge representation. This product can be purchased for between $5,000 and $10,000.

CALIFORNIA INTELLIGENCE
(415) 391–4846

Xsys
The Xsys product was implemented using LISP. Xsys sells for $995.

CARNEGIE GROUP, INC.
(412) 642–6900

Knowledge Craft
The Knowledge Craft was implemented using Common LISP. It utilizes frame-based, semantic network, frames, logic representation, and production systems methods for its knowledge representation. Knowledge Craft sells between $9,500 and $72,500.

COMPUTER THOUGHT CORP.
(214) 424–2511

OPS5 + with C interface
The OPS5 + with C interface product is implemented using C. It uses rule-based methods for its knowledge representation. OPS5 + with C interface sells for $1,800.

COMPUTER SOFTWARE MANAGEMENT & INFORMATION CENTER (COSMIC)
(404) 542–3265

Aesop
The Aesop product is implemented using Franz LISP. It uses logic-based methods for its knowledge representation. This product sells for $300.

Cerberus
The Cerberus product is implemented using Fortran 77. It utilizes logical rule-based methods with associated levels of confidence for its knowledge representation. This products sells for $1,750.

Star
The Star product is implemented using C. It uses network methods for its knowledge representation. This product sells for $2,000.

Clips
The Clips product is implemented using C. It uses pattern matching methods for its knowledge representation. The Clips product sells for $200.

CULLINET SOFTWARE, INC.
(617) 329–7700

Application Expert
The Application Expert product is implemented using Cobol. It uses rule-based methods for its knowledge representation. The Application Expert sells between $14,000 and $60,000.

DIGITAL EQUIPMENT CORPORATION
(617) 490–0111

VAX OPS5
VAX OPS5 is implemented using BLISS. It uses rule-based methods for its knowledge representation. This product sells between $2,000 and $8,000.

DYNACOMP, INC.
(716) 265–4040

Hansen-Predict

The Hansen-Predict product is implemented using machine language. It uses rule-based methods for its knowledge representation. This product sells for $99.95.

DYNAMIC MASTER SYSTEMS, INC.
(404) 565–0771

Topsi

The Topsi product is implemented using C. It uses rules-based methods for its knowledge representation. The Topsi product sells for $250.

EXPERTECH
(702) 831–0136

XI Plus

The XI Plus is implemented using Prolog and C. It utilizes rule, fact, question, query-based, demon and default methods for its knowledge representation. This products sells for $1,250.

EXPERTELLIGENCE, INC.
(805) 969–7871

Expercommon OPS5

The Expercommon OPS5 product is implemented using Common LISP. It uses rule-based methods for its knowledge representation. The Expercommon OPS5 sells for $625.

Experfacts

The Experfacts product is implemented using Experlisp 1.5. It uses rule-based methods for its knowledge representation. This product sells for $495.

ExperOPS5 Plus

The ExperOPS5 Plus product is implemented using Experlisp 1.5. It uses rule-based methods for its knowledge representation. The ExperOPS5 product sells for $495.

EXPERT SYSTEMS INTERNATIONAL
(215) 735–8510

ESP Advisor
The ESP Advisor product is implemented using Prolog. It uses rule based methods for its knowledge representation. This product sells for $895.

ESP FrameEngine
The ESP FrameEngine product is implemented using Prolog. It uses rule and frame based methods for its knowledge representation. This product sells for $895.00

EXSYS, INC.
(505) 836–6676

Expert System Development Package
The Expert System Development Package is implemented using C. It uses rule-based methods for its knowledge representation. The Expert System Development Package sells from $395.

GENSYM CORP.
(617) 547–9606

G2
The G2 product is implemented using Common LISP. It uses rule-based methods for its knowledge representation. The G2 product sells for $36,000.

GOLD HILL COMPUTERS, INC.
(617) 492–2071

Goldworks
The Goldworks product is implemented using GC LISP. It utilizes frame-based, multiple inheritance lattice and multiple values for slots for its knowledge representation. Goldworks sells for $7,500.

HONEYWELL BULL, INC.
(617) 895–6000

Idothea
The Idothea product is implemented using Common LISP. It uses Logic, frame and rule-based methods for its knowledge representation.

INFERENCE CORP.
(213) 417–7997

Automated Reasoning Tool
The Automated Reasoning Tool is implemented using LISP. It uses rule-based methods for its knowledge representation. This product sells between $29,500 and $60,000.

INFORMATION BUILDERS, INC.
(212) 736–4433

Level 5
The Level 5 product is implemented using Proprietary Language. It uses rule-based methods for its knowledge representation. The Level 5 product sells between $456 and $685.

INTELLICORP
(415) 965–5500

Knowledge Engineering Environment
The Knowledge Engineering Environment is implemented using LISP. It utilizes frame, rule-based, object-oriented programming and assumption-based truth maintenance for its knowledge representation. The Knowledge Engineering Environment sells for $55,000.

INTELLIGENCEWARE, INC.
(213) 417–8896

Intelligence / Compiler
The Intelligence/Compiler product is implemented using C. It uses Frame, logic and rule based methods for its knowledge representation. This products sells for $490.

JEFFREY PERRONE & ASSOCIATES, INC.
(415) 431-9562

Expert-Ease
The Expert-Ease product is implemented using Pascal. It uses example-based methods for its knowledge representation. The Expert-Ease product sells for $695.

Expert Edge
The Expert Edge product is implemented using Pascal. It uses rule-based methods for its knowledge representation. The product sells for $1,495.

KDS CORP.
(312) 251–2621

KDS 3+
The KDS 3+ product is implemented using Assembler. It utilizes object-oriented and example-based methods for its knowledge representation. This product sells for $1,495.

LIGHTWAVE, INC.
(813) 988–5033

Expert System Inference Engine
The Expert System Inference Engine is implemented using Pascal. It uses the IF-THEN method for its knowledge representation. The Expert System Inference Engine sells for $144.

MACHINE INTELLIGENCE CORP.
(516) 589–1676

Wizdom
The Wizdom product uses fact-based methods for its knowledge representation. This product sells from $85.

MDBS, INC.
(317) 463–2581

Guru
The Guru product is implemented using Lattice C. It uses rule-based methods for its knowledge representation. This product sells from $6,500.

MILLER MICROCOMPUTER SERVICES
(617) 653–6136

Expert-2
The Expert-2 product is implemented using MMS Forth. It uses rule-based and consequent reasoning methods for its knowledge representation. This product sells from $250 including MMS Forth.

MOUNTAIN VIEW PRESS, INC.
(415) 961–4103

MVP-Forth Expert 2
The MVP-Forth Expert 2 is implemented using Forth. It uses rule-based methods as its knowledge representation. This product sells for $150.

NEURON DATA, INC.
(415) 321–4488

Nexpert Object
The Nexpert Object is implemented using C. It uses rule and object based methods for its knowledge representation. The Nexpert Object sells between $5,000 and $10,000.

NIXDORF COMPUTER AG
(617) 890–3600

Twaice
The Twaice product is implemented using Prolog. It uses rule-based methods for its knowledge representation. This product sells for $35,000.

PAPERBACK SOFTWARE INTERNATIONAL
(415) 644–2116

VP-Expert
The VP-Expert is implemented using Proprietary. It uses rule-based methods for its knowledge representation. The VP-Expert sells for $124.95.

PAR TECHNOLOGY CORP.
(315) 738–0600

ERS
The ERS product is implemented using C. It utilizes Inference Network for its knowledge representation. This product sells for $2,000.

PERSONAL COMPUTER ENGINEERS, INC.
(213) 757–7537

Knowledge-Oriented Programming System (KOPS)/Dbase
The Knowledge-Oriented Programming System is coded in Dbase. It uses rule-based methods for its knowledge representation. This product sells for $75.

KOPS/FW2
The KOPS/FW2 product is implemented in Proprietary. It uses rule-based methods for its knowledge representation. This product sells for $100.

PREDICTION SYSTEMS, INC.
(201) 223–5000

General Simulation System
The General Simulation System is implemented in Proprietary. The system sells from $19,000.

PRODUCTION SYSTEMS TECHNOLOGIES, INC.
(412) 683–4000

OPS83
The OPS83 product is implemented using C. It uses rule-based

methods for its knowledge representation. The OSP83 sells between $1,950 and $20,000.

PROGRAMMING LOGIC SYSTEMS, INC.
(203) 877–7988

Augmented Prolog for Expert Systems
The Augmented Prolog for Expert Systems is implemented using Micro Prolog. It uses rule-based methods for its knowledge representation. This product sells from $99.

PROGRAMS IN MOTION
(617) 358–7722

First Class, First Class Fusion
The First Class, First class Fusion is implemented using Pascal and some assembler. It utilizes inductive, example-based and rule entry optional for its knowledge representation. This product sells between $495 and $1,295.

RADIAN CORP.
(512) 454–4797

Rulemaster 2
The Rulemaster 2 is implemented in C. It uses rule and example-based methods for its knowledge representation. This product sells between $495 and $28,000.

SMART COMMUNICATIONS, INC.
(212) 486–1894

Smart Expert Editor
The Smart Expert Editor is implemented using C. It uses rule-based methods for its knowledge representation. This product sells between $4,500 and $12,500.

Smart Translator
The Smart Translator is implemented using C. It uses rule-based methods for its knowledge representation. This product sells between $38,500 and $85,000.

SOFTSYNC, INC.
(212) 685–2080

Superexpert
The Superexpert product is implemented using Forth and Pascal. It utilizes example-based methods for its knowledge representation. The Superexpert sells for $199.95.

SOFTWARE AE, INC.
(703) 527–4344

Knowledge Engineering System
The Knowledge Engineering System is implemented using C. It uses object-oriented and rule-based methods, production rules, subsystem, hypothesis and test subsystem and bayes subsystem for its knowledge representation. This system sells between $4,000 and $60,000.

SYSTEMS RESEARCH LABORATORIES, INC.
(513) 426–6000

Dexpert
The Dexpert product is implemented using LISP. It uses production systems methods for its knowledge representation. This product sells for $3,500.

TEKNOWLEDGE, INC.
(415) 424–9955

Copernicus
The Copernicus product is implemented using C. It utilizes logic, fact and frame based methods, and production systems for its knowledge representation. This product sells between $12,000 and $45,000.

S.1
The S.1 product is implemented using C. It uses rule, fact and frame based and production systems methods for its knowledge representation. The S.1 product sells between $9,000 and 25,000.

M.1

The M.1 product is implemented using C. It uses logic, rule, fact, relation based, and production systems methods for its knowledge representation. This product sells for $5,000.

TEXAS INSTRUMENTS, INC.
(800) 527–3500

Personal Consultant Series

The Personal Consultant Series is implemented using LISP and C. It utilizes frame and rule-based methods for its knowledge representation. The Personal Consultant Series sells between $495 and $2,950.

UNISYS CORP.
(313) 972–7000

KES II

The KES II product is implemented using C. It uses product rule, frame-based, classes and inheritance, and demons for its knowledge representation. The product sells between $2,000 and $29,000.

KEE / PC-to-Host

The KEE/PC-to-Host product is implemented using LISP. It uses frame based and production systems methods for its knowledge representation. The product sells for $49,500.

Glossary

Agenda — In inference engine based systems it is common that more than one rule has all its left hand side clauses true at a given point in time. These rules are posted to an agenda mechanism waiting for conflict resolution to take place. The conflict resolution process selects one of the rules which is currently on the agenda for subsequent execution. That rule then has its right hand side executed. The result of this process is a state transition in the knowledge base leading to a new agenda where the process begins again.

Alarm management — In a plant today, multiple alarms are usually signaled at the same time. This is due to the effects of process interactions, as well as the surrounding control structures which are implemented in a real plant environment. Alarm Management refers to the problem of being able to diagnose what the cause of a particular malfunction is given that one or more alarms have been signaled. Once this diagnostic capability has been performed, an alarm management system would provide a recommendation in terms of treatment for the underlying problem. Some underlying management systems also provide for an analysis component to improve subsequent alarm handling.

Algorithm — A procedure or methodology by which one can structure the overall solution to a problem. Artificial Intelligence and expert systems requires the intelligent use of open algorithms. In traditional computing, an algorithm is usually of the closed form analytic type. In expert systems or knowledge bases, the algorithm is usually more open and relies to some extent on search and heuristics to arrive at the solution. However, unless there is a clean specification of the starting point, the ending point and the navigational mechanism used to arrive at a solution, a knowledge base will inefficiently use computes to solve the problem. A well defined knowledge base should have a clearly defined heuristic algorithm which will allow it to focus its attention in an intelligent fashion thus arriving at a solution efficiently. Most knowledge based applications use a subtle combination of traditional analytic algorithms intermixed in a mixed computing initiative with heuristic open algorithms.

Artificial intelligence — Artificial Intelligence is a set of tools, concepts, techniques and methodologies which allows one to model and computerize non-closed form analytic problems. Inherently, its application is geared towards addressing issues which cannot be specified using purely traditional mathematical analysis and systems engineering approaches. These flexible modeling and computerization techniques allows under certain circumstances the capturing of skill, judgement and expertise. Moreover, facilities such as learning, justification and explanation become natural when built on top of the paradigms associated with AI. Inherently, AI is used to capture physics associated with the solution to a problem which requires highly flexible representation, as well as computation. If there is no physics associated with the problem, then AI is reduced to the lowly state of simply having to unintelligently search for a possible solution. To the extent that there is physics, the AI paradigms and methodologies can model in an intelligent fashion the non-well formed aspects of problems, integrating them into an intelligent overall algorithmic approach and solution in a knowledge based format.

Backward chaining — Backward chaining is a paradigm of intelligent reasoning which allows one to assert an unproven hypothesis and then search backwards for the facts that would prove it. Many problems can be solved intelligently using a backward chaining mode of intelligent reasoning. In addition, one can view backward chaining as a methodology to obtain on demand computation in a knowledge based environment.

Client server — A methodology and technique for establishing sophisticated distributed communications between multiple processes which are executing on one or more computational environments. It is through this paradigm that one can accomplish sophisticated symbolic distributed artificial intelligence, in a way that is naturally supportable on traditional hardware platforms utilizing traditional low level communication constructs. This paradigm can be implemented to include the facilities of high availability and fault tolerance. Moreover, it can be extended to allow sophisticated peer to peer communications to take place between multiple knowledge bases, as well as traditional computing facilities across an arbitrary network of computers.

Cooperating expert systems — A methodology for the decomposition of a knowledge based application into multiple peer processes. In addition, a strategy for conflict resolution between the cooperating agents with respect to the overall solution of a problem. Cooperating expert systems as a philosophy and methodology of computation is in direct contrast to the big expert system approach. It is a method which allows a phased implementation approach, as well as maintainability and high performance utilizing the overall automation environment. The conflict resolution strategies including cooperating, collaborating, meta and end user overrides are geared to providing a high degree of parallelism between the agents while guaranteeing a meaningful solution to a particular problem.

Collaboration mode — A more sophisticated mode of conflict resolution between peer cooperating agents when the cooperating mode fails to produce a satisfactory resolution. In the collaboration mode, the peer agents enter into an explicit bidirectional dialogue to arbitrate a solution to the conflict in a way that is at least feasible if not optimal.

Conflict resolution — In a single expert system that is implemented in an inference engine architecture, this term commonly refers to selecting a given rule for execution, given that more than one rule is true at a given point in time. This might best be termed conflict resolution within an expert system. When the problem is being solved in a cooperating expert system format, then there is a higher form of conflict resolution. That form of conflict resolution is between two or more of the cooperating expert systems. When this occurs, arbitration is necessary to arrive at a consistent decision which is at least feasible for the conflicting agents involved, if not indeed optimal.

Cooperating mode — In the architecture, design and implementation of a cooperating expert system environment, the first and most straight forward mode of conflict resolution is the cooperating mode. In this mode, the peer cooperating agents try to live with the decisions made by other expert systems and treat those decisions as constraints to their intelligent processing of the problem. This is accomplished by including a constraint propagation model for all of the experts in any given expert systems.

Data driven computation — In traditional programming environments, the logic finds the data. This results in an extensive and highly complex control and computational structure. Many AI environments provide a structure by which the data finds the logic. This inversion of the normal programming construct leads to a somewhat simpler overall flow of control in the architecture, design and implementation of an application. Inherently, it is the methodology of data driven computation that is utilized in constructing a solution which relies on opportunistic programming. Data driven environments are particularly useful in implementing event driven systems.

Declarative component — A knowledge base is comprised of two components, the declarative component and the procedural component. The declarative component contains the data and representation model in a format that the logic base can operate over. Typically, one uses fact patterns, schemas, frames, objects, semantic networks and inheritance taxonomies to comprise this aspect of the knowledge base. Good knowledge base design in most applications usually results in extensive use of declarative modeling. It keeps the data and representation in this component as powerful and expressive as possible while making the operators which comprise the logic base as simple and straightforward as possible.

Distributed artificial intelligence — The set of tools, methodologies, techniques and paradigms associated with relaxing the single CPU model of knowledge based execution. In the real world, performance is key. In addition, it becomes necessary in some problem domains to guarantee a fail soft if not a fault tolerant environment. Distributed AI allows the utilization of multiple CPUs to arrive intelligently at an overall solution to the problem.

The knowledge bases can be intelligently distributed over the network along with the required traditional computing facilities.

Domain — Domain refers to a particular application area described by a particular collection of procedures, algorithms, data, representation, knowledge and rules.

Domain dependent solution shell — A methodology and set of techniques which allows the building of a flexible, intelligent and parametric application for a specific domain. An example would be an intelligent scheduling system for the manufacturing industries. A domain dependent solution shell is easily customizable and parameterizable by the end user without any need for artificial intelligence or expert system knowledge. Moreover, all the technical details of traditional computer science had been abstracted away in the routine installation, use and maintenance of the shell by the end user.

Expert system — An intelligent automation environment comprised of traditional, as well as heuristic methods in solving a particular problem. The term expert system is quite often synonymously used with the term knowledge base. When a particular expert system has a large AI content, that AI content will usually involve the modeling of the skill, judgement and expertise of human beings in solving problems in a particular domain.

Forward chaining — A methodology of intelligent reasoning utilized in the building of expert system and knowledge based applications. It is a method by which a problem is solved by reasoning from facts to draw conclusions.

Garbage — Garbage is an undesirable side effect when LISP objects are present in a LISP environment that are unreferenced and serve no useful purpose. At an appropriate time these unused or unreferenced objects must be garbage collected to be available for reallocation as processing continues.

Global knowledge base — Overwhelmingly, most expert system shells execute in the virtual address space of a computer. The knowledge base which is comprised of both declarative and procedural representation is short lived when compared to traditional database systems. A global knowledge base represents the implementation of a stable storage architecture residing on the file system of a particular computer, to implement in a more permanent fashion, the in memory knowledge base. Presently, relational database technology is an ideal candidate to implement a global knowledge base in an intelligent fashion. Relational databases marry very well with present expert system shell technology and provide a convenient vehicle for being able to save state, as well as long term declarative and procedural knowledge.

Heuristic — A broad-based term, usually referring to a rule of thumb. In general, a heuristic is a piece of logic utilizable in the solution to a problem which cannot be modeled as a closed form analytic expression. It usually results from the skill, judgement or expertise of a particular human expert.

Hypothetical reasoning — A methodology by which a knowledge base can explore multiple worlds in parallel while attempting to solve a particular problem. Each of these worlds are developed and contrasted with other possible solution approaches. Eventually, a hypothetical world becomes a candidate for the solution to the problem.

Inference — A mechanism usually associated with the application of rules to declarative knowledge in a knowledge base. It is commonly modeled by an "IF-THEN" type of format.

Inheritance — Inheritance is a mechanism by which specific nodes obtain their qualities and values from less specific nodes in a tree type of structure. For instance, higher up in the inheritance taxonomy we will tend to talk about classes where lower down in the taxonomy we will model and capture instance structures. An inheritance taxonomy and an inheritance mechanism is an efficient way to structure the declarative component of a knowledge base. Many problems in the real world can be conveniently modeled and organized in this format. Quite often, computational and modeling simplifications will result from an intelligent use of this technique.

Integrated AI — A set of tools, concepts and methodologies which allows one to subtly combine the world of heuristic computing with the world of traditional computing. An example would be the tight coupling of a knowledge base with a traditional relational database. Most real world problems are best served by solving them in an integrated AI format on traditional architectures. This results in an overall high performance solution, full featured, while minimizing the time to development, as well as the development costs. It is through the techniques associated with integrated AI that a computing environment such as the VAX can be fully exploited to solve state of the art knowledge based problems in a meaningful fashion.

Knowledge base — A heuristic data base usually comprised of structured declarative knowledge, as well as structured procedural knowledge. It is a term that is quite often synonymously used with the term expert system. The declarative knowledge is usually comprised of fact patterns, schemas, frames, inheritance taxonomies and the like. The procedural component or the logic base is usually comprised of such entities as rules, scripts, methods and demons.

Knowledge engineer — Commonly referred to as a person who implements an expert system. This individual is knowledgeable in AI tools, concepts, paradigms and methodologies. In addition, he is skilled in the interviewing and structuring process necessary to arrive at a solid expert system format and solution. This usually results in the knowledge engineer working with one or more domain experts.

Logical dependency — When a given fact or assertion is dependent upon a prior fact or assertion then a logical dependency exists between these two facts or assertions. If we were to retract the earlier fact then logically we should retract the subsequent fact or facts. Inherently, logical dependencies represent a mechanism by which we can do automatic restructuring of the knowledge base in an efficient manner without having to fire many rules or execute many procedures to clean up the environment after a particular assertion, fact or state of the world no longer exists.

Logic base — The logic base represents the operators of a heuristically architected, designed and implemented knowledge base. It is usually comprised of such entities as rules, scripts, methods, demons and procedures. It is the logic base that allows a state transition to take place in the solution to a problem. The logic base operates over the declarative component of the knowledge base. In a typical data driven inference engine environment, the inference engine performs the functionality of applying the operators over the declarative representation.

Meta — Meta is defined as the operating system to an application. In the single expert system approach, meta provides the access to system services for the rest of the application and any coordination that is deemed necessary to intelligently solve the problem. In a cooperating expert system environment, meta provides the services of higher order conflict resolution when the cooperating and collaboration modes fail to produce a satisfactory result. Essentially, meta can be viewed as the Chairman of the Board in a cooperating expert system context. It is attempting to intelligently arbitrate discrepancies and conflicts between the multiple agents. This facility leads to intelligent and efficient pseudo parallel processing by the agents in the solution to a particular instance of a problem. Essentially, meta is responsible for the heuristic solution to an N person non-zero sum game where each game player is one of the cooperating agents. If appropriate, it is meta who will decide when a human end user of the application is necessary to arbitrate a conflict. Under this set of circumstances, meta will intelligently involve a human being, present the alternatives and solicit direction and advice in resolving the conflict between two or more peer cooperating agents.

Rule — A common methodology for capturing procedural knowledge and encoding it into an expert system application. Rules usually form a majority of the logic base when a typical production rule system is built. Often, rules follow a common "IF-THEN" format when utilized in capturing heuristic knowledge associated with a particular problem.

Scheduling — Scheduling is the problem of optimally allocating resources given a set of constraints imposed by the general manufacturing environment. Inherently, it is a complicated optimization problem which is critical to the daily routine of life in most manufacturing environments. Historically, scheduling has been accomplished by utilizing traditional operations research techniques such as linear programming. It is a natural application area for the use of AI tools, concepts and techniques.

Schema — A schema is an example of a structure used in building the declarative component of a knowledge base. A schema allows the capturing of the attributes of a given entity or class of entities along with their specific values. More importantly, a schema provides for the mechanisms necessary to describe the relationships between itself and other schemata. A schema system is a convenient facility for capturing not only the data associated with structures but their representation and relationships as well. Schemas are usually comprised of slots which are simple placeholding mechanisms for defining attributes, relationships, as well as methods and appending specific values to them.

Time-critical artificial intelligence — A set of tools, concepts, techniques and methodologies which allows a knowledge base to explicitly reason about time in the solution of a problem. Fundamentally, most problems are dynamical and have underlying time constants associated with their solution. Time critical AI allows one to model the time constants, build a time constraint propagation model and then devise knowledge intensive search strategies to solve a problem. It is important to reason how intelligent an expert system needs to be versus how intelligent an expert system can afford to be. Usually, time critical AI results in having multiple bifurcating search strategies, one or more geared for arriving at a feasible decision and one or more geared for subsequently arriving at an optimal decision if time permits.

Tuning — A problem that is omnipresent in the process control industries resulting from the need to parametrically optimize traditional control structures such as proportional integral derivative control laws. The optimal values of the parameters of any given loop are dependent on the state of the manufacturing process, the goals of goodness of tuning, the characteristics and quality of the feedstocks, as well as the nature and effect of disturbances entering the manufacturing environment. The PID control laws are typically implemented on traditional control system products such as single loop instruments, programmable logic controllers and distributed control systems. Tuning of process control laws is an excellent industrial problem to apply AI tools, concepts and techniques to.

Uncertainty — A state of the world that derives from an incomplete description and a lack of total determinism with respect to a particular problem. This might result from either stochastic elements being present, fuzzy models or incomplete specifications of the problem. Expert system technology is particularly adapt at modeling and handling uncertainty in a consistent fashion which is flexible and automatable.

Bibliography

Arden, Bruce W., Editor. *What Can Be Automated?* The MIT Press, 1983.

Abelson, Harold, Sussman, Gerald Jay, Sussman, Julie. *Structure and Interpretation of Computer Programs.* The MIT Press, McGraw-Hill, 1985.

Allen, John. *Anatomy of LISP.* McGraw-Hill, 1970.

Astrom, Karl J., Wittenmark, Bjorn. *Computer Controlled Systems, Theory and Design.* Prentice-Hall 1984.

Barstow, David R. *Knowledge-Based Program Construction.* Elsevier North Holland, Inc. 1979.

Bauer, F.L., Dennis, J.B., Goos, G., Gotlieb, C.C., Graham, R.M., Griffiths, M., Helms, H.J., Morton, B., Poole, P.C., Tsichritzis, D., Waite, W.M. *Software Engineering, An Advanced Course.* Springer-Verlag, 1977.

Bolter, David J. *Turing's Man, Western Culture in the Computer Age.* The University of North Carolina Press, 1984.

Boehm, Barry W. *Software Engineering Economics.* Prentice-Hall, Inc., 1981.

Brownston, Lee, Farrell, Robert, Kant, Elaine, Martin, Nancy. *Programming Expert Systems in OPS5, An Introduction to Rule-Based Programming.* Addison-Wesley, 1985.

Buchanan, Bruce G., Shortliffe, Edward H. *Rule-Based Expert Systems*. Addison-Wesley, October, 1984.

Cero, Stefano, Pelagatti, Giuseppe. *Distributed Databases, Principals & Systems*. McGraw-Hill, 1984.

Caianiello, E.R., Musso, G., Editors. *Cybernetic Systems: Recognition, Learning, Self-Organisation*. Research Studies Press Ltd., John Wiley & Sons, Inc., 1984.

Charniak, Eugene, McDermott, Drew. *Introduction to Artificial Intelligence*. Addison-Wesley, 1985.

Charniak, Eugene., Riesbeck, Christopher K., McDermott, Drew V. *Artificial Intelligence Programming*. Lawrence Erlbaum Associates, 1980.

Clocksin, W.F., Mellish C.S. *Programming in Prolog, Second Edition*. Springer-Verlag, 1984.

Cohen, Paul R., Feigenbaum, Edward A. *The Handbook of Artificial Intelligence, Vol. 1*. William Kaufmann, Inc., 1982.

Cohen, Paul R., Feigenbaum, Edward A. *The Handbook of Artificial Intelligence, Vol. 2*. William Kaufmann, Inc., 1982.

Cohen, Paul R., Feigenbaum, Edward A. *The Handbook of Artificial Intelligence, Vol. 3*. William Kaufmann, Inc., 1982.

Cohen, Paul R. *Heuristic Reasoning about Uncertainty: An Artificial Intelligence Approach*. Pitman Publishing Limited, 1985.

Cox, Brad J. *Object Oriented Programming, An Evolutionary Approach*. Addison-Wesley, 1986.

Cullingford, Richard E. *Natural Language Processing*. Roman & Littlefield, 1986.

Date, C.J. *An Introduction to Database Systems, Vol. 1, Fourth Edition*. Addison-Wesley Systems Programming Series. 1986.

Date, C.J. *An Introduction to Database Systems, Vol. 2.* Addison-Wesley Systems Programming Series. 1983

Date, C.J. *Relational Database, Selected Writings.* Addison-Wesley Publishing Company, 1986.

Davis, Randall, Lenat, Douglas B. *Knowledge-Based Systems in Artificial Intelligence.* McGraw-Hill, 1982.

Deshpande, Pradeep B., Ash, Raymond H. *Elements of Computer Process Control, with Advanced Control Applications.* Instrument Society of America, 1981.

Dyer, Michael G. *In-Depth Understanding, A Computer Model of Integrated Processing for Narrative Comprehension.* The MIT Press, 1983. Fandal, Gunther., Spronk, Jaap, Editors. *Multiple Criteria Decision Methods and Applications.* Springer-Verlag 1985

Forsyth, Richard. *Expert Systems, Principles and Case Studies.* Chapman and Hall, 1984.

Fortier, Paul J. *Design and Analysis of Distributed Real-Time Systems.* Intertext Publications/McGraw Hill, 1985.

Fortier, Paul J. *Design of Distributed Operating Systems, Concepts and Technology.* Intertext Publications/McGraw Hill, 1985.

Gevarter, William B. *Artificial Intelligence Expert Systems Computer Vision and Natural Language Processing.* Noyes Publications, 1984.

Glorioso, Robert M., Osorio, Fernando C. Colon. *Engineering Intelligent Systems, Concepts, Theory and Applications.* Digital Equipment Corporation, 1980.

Harmon, Paul, King, David. *Artificial Intelligence in Business, Expert Systems.* John Wiley & Sons, Inc. 1985.

Haugeland, John. *Artificial Intelligence, The Very Idea.* The MIT Press, 1985.

Hayes-Roth, Frederick, Waterman, Donald A., Lenat, Douglas, B. *Building Expert Systems*. Addison-Wesley, 1983.

Hayes, J.E., Michie D. *Intelligent Systems, the Unprecedented Opportunity*. Ellis Horwood Limited. 1984.

Hillier, Federick S., Lieberman, Gerald J. *Introduction to Operations Research*. Holden-Day, Inc., 1980.

Hillis, Daniel W. *The Connection Machine*. The MIT Press, 1985.

Holtz, Frederick. *LISP, The Language of Artificial Intelligence*. Tab Books, Inc., 1985.

Keeney, Ralph L., Raiffa, Howard. *Decisions with Multiple Objectives: Preferences and Value Tradeoffs*. John Wiley & Sons, 1976.

Kolodner, Janet L. *Retrieval and Organizational Strategies in Conceptual Memory: A Computer Model*. Lawrence Erlbaum Associates, Pub. 1984.

Knuth, Donald E. *Fundamental Algorithms, Vol. 1*. Addison-Wesley, 1973.

Knuth, Donald E. *Seminumerical Algorithms, Vol. 2*. Addison-Wesley, 1973.

Knuth, Donald E. *Sorting and Searching, Vol. 3*. Addison-Wesley, 1973.

Korf, Richard E. *Learning to Solve Problems by Searching for Macro-Operations*. Pitman Publishing Limited, 1985.

McCorduck, Pamela. *Machines Who Think*. W.H. Freeman and Company, 1979.

McMillan, Gregory K. *Tuning and Control Loop Performance, Monograph Series 4*. Instrument Society of America, 1983.

Melnyk, Steven A., Carter, Phillip L., Dilts, David M., Lyth, David M. *Shop Floor Control*. Dow Jones-Irwin, American Production and Inventory Control Society, 1985.

Michalski, Ryszard S., Carbonell, Jamie, G., Mitchell, Tom M. *Machine Learning, An Artificial Intelligence Approach*. Tioga Publishing Company, 1983.

Michie, Donald. *Machine Intelligence and Related Topics*. Gordon and Breach Science Publishers, 1982.

Miller, Perry L. *A Critiquing Approach to Expert Computer Advice: Attending*. Pitman Publishing, 1984.

Murrill, Paul W. *Fundamentals of Process Control Theory*, Instrument Society of America, 1981.

Negoita, Virgil Constantine. *Expert Systems and Fuzzy Systems*. The Benjamin/Cummings Publishing Company, 1985.

Nilsson, Nils J. *Principles of Artificial Intelligence*. Tioga Publishing Company, 1980.

Nilsson, Nils J. *Problem-Solving Methods in Artificial Intelligence*. McGraw-Hill, 1971.

Ogata, Katsuhilo. *Modern Control Engineering*, Prentice-Hall, Inc., 1970.

Ohta, Yuichi. *Knowledge-Based Interpretation of Outdoor Natural Color Scenes*. Pitman Publishing Limited, 1985.

Orlicky, Joseph. *Material Requirements Planning, The New Way of Life in Production and Inventory Management*. McGraw Hill, 1975

O'Shea, Tim. *Advances in Artificial Intelligence*. Elsevier Science Publishers, 1985.

Osherson, Daniel N., Stob, Michael., Weinstein, Scott. *Systems That Learn*. The MIT Press, 1986.

Palay, Andrew J. *Searching with Probabilities*. Pitman Publishing Limited, 1985.

Papoulis, Athanasios. *Probability, Random Variables, and Stochastic Processes, Second Edition*. McGraw-Hill, 1984.

Patrick, Edward A., Fattu, James, M. *Artificial Intelligence with Statistical Pattern Recognition*. Prentice-Hall, 1986.

Pearl, J., Editor. *Search and Heuristics*. North-Holland Publishing, 1983.

Politakis, Peter G. *Empirical Analysis for Expert Systems*. Pitman Publishing Limited, 1985.

Pylyshyn, Zenon W. *Computation and Cognition*. A Bradford Book, The MIT Press, 1985.

Queinnec, Christian. *LISP*. John Wiley & Sons, 1984.

Rauch-Hindin, Wendy B. *Artificial Intelligence in Business, Science, and Industry, Vol. 1, Fundamentals*. Prentice-Hall, 1986.

Rauch-Hindin, Wendy B. *Artificial Intelligence in Business, Science, and Industry, Vol. 2, Applications*. Prentice-Hall, 1985.

Rich, Elaine. *Artificial Intelligence*. McGraw-Hill, 1983.

Sager, Naomi. *Natural Language Informaton Processing*. Addison-Wesley, 1981.

Schank, Roger C., Childers, Peter. *The Cognitive Computer on Language, Learning and Artificial Intelligence*. Roger C. Schank, 1984.

Schildt, Herbert. *Artificial Intelligence, Using C*. Osborne McGraw-Hill, 1987.

Schroeder, Roger G. *Operations Management, Decision Maning in the Operations Function, Second Edition*. McGraw-Hill, 1985.

Silver, B. *Meta-Level Inference*. Elsevier Science Pub., 1986.

Simon, Herbert A. *The Sciences of the Artificial, The Second Edition.* The MIT Press, 1984.

Slemaker, Chuck M. *The Principles & Practice of Cost Schedule Control Systems.* Petrocelli Books, Inc. Princeton, NJ, 1985.

Steele, Guy L., Jr. *Common Lisp, Reference Manual.* Digital Equipment Corporation, 1983.

Stephanopoulos, George. *Chemical Process Control, An Introduction to Theory and Practice.* Prentice-Hall, 1984.

Steuer, Ralph E. *Multiple Criteria Optimization: Theory, Computation and Application.* John Wiley and Sons, 1986.

Teorey, Toby J., Fry, James P. *Design of Database Structures.* Prentice-Hall, Inc., Englewood Cliffs, NJ. 1982.

Vollmann, Thomas E., Berry, William L., Whybark, Clay D. *Manufacturing Planning and Control Systems.* Dow Jones-Irwin, Homewood, Illinois, 1984.

Warnecke, H.J., Steinhilper, R. *Flexible Manufacturing Systems.* IFS Publications, Ltd., 1985.

Waterman, D.A., Hayes-Roth, Frederick. *Pattern-Directed Inference Systems.* Academic Press, Inc. 1978.

Winston, Patrick Henry, Brown, Richard Henry. *Artificial Intelligence: An MIT Perspective, Vol. 1.* The MIT Press, 1979.

Weiss, Sholom M., Kulikowski, Casimir A. *A Practical Guide to Designing Expert Systems.* Rowman & Allanheld, 1984.

Wiener, Norbert. *Cybernetics.* The MIT Press, 1948 and 1961.

Wilensky, Robert. *Planning and Understanding, A Computational Approach to Human Reasoning.* Addison-Wesley, 1983.

Winograd, Terry. *Understanding Natural Language.* Academic Press, 1972.

Winston, Patrick Henry, Horn, Berthold Klaus Paul. *LISP, Second Edition*. Addison-Wesley, 1984.

Winston, Patrick Henry, Brown, Richard Henry, Editors. *Artificial Intelligence: An MIT Perspective*. The MIT Press, 1979.

Winston, Patrick Henry. Artificial Intelligence, Second Edition. *Addison-Wesley, 1984*.

Wos, Larry, Overbeek, Ross, Lusk, Ewing, Boyle, Jim. *Automated Reasoning, Introduction and Applications*. Prentice-Hall, 1984.

Index